C3P3 Leadership

C3P3 Leadership

A Framework for High-Impact
Leadership, Strategy, and Performance

Andrew F Middleton

Published by Andrew F Middleton
Copyright © 2025 Andrew F Middleton
First published May 2025

All rights reserved. No part of this publication may be reproduced, stored in a retrieval system or transmitted in any form or by any means, electronic, mechanical, photocopying, recording or otherwise, without the prior written permission of the publisher.

Disclaimer

The information contained in this book, *C3P3 Leadership: A Framework for High-Impact Leadership, Strategy & Performance*, is provided for general informational and educational purposes only. The content reflects the personal views and experiences of the author and does not constitute professional advice, including but not limited to legal, financial or psychological advice. Readers should seek independent professional advice tailored to their specific circumstances before acting on any information contained in this book.

The author makes no representations or warranties of any kind, express or implied, about the completeness, accuracy, reliability, suitability, or availability of the information contained in this book. Any reliance placed on such information is strictly at the reader's own risk.

References to third-party works, quotes, models, or brand names are used for illustrative purposes only. All intellectual property rights remain with their respective owners. The inclusion of such references does not imply endorsement, affiliation, or sponsorship by the referenced entities.

The views expressed in this book are solely those of the author and do not represent the views of any government entity or department. The author has taken care to ensure compliance with confidentiality obligations under the Defence Act 1903 (Cth); however, no classified or sensitive information is disclosed in this book.

This book discusses mental health struggles, including references to post-traumatic stress disorder (PTSD) and suicide. Readers who may find these topics distressing are encouraged to proceed with caution and seek support if needed.

If you or someone you know is struggling, please contact a mental health professional or a support service in your area. In Australia, you can contact Lifeline at 13 11 14 for confidential support 24/7.

While every effort has been made to ensure the accuracy of the information provided, the author disclaims all liability for any loss or damage arising directly or indirectly from the use of this book or its contents.

By purchasing or reading this book, you agree that the author will not be held liable for any actions taken based on the information provided herein.

ISBN: 978-1-7641071-0-5 (pbk) 978-1-7641071-1-2 (ebook)

 A catalogue record for this book is available from the National Library of Australia

ACKNOWLEDGEMENTS

I want to express my deepest gratitude to my partner, Shelley. Shelley is a true leader in every sense of the word—strong, compassionate, and unwaveringly supportive. Throughout the journey of writing this book, Shelley has been my cornerstone. She reviewed my work with a keen eye, provided critical and constructive feedback, and challenged me to refine my ideas, ensuring this book became the best it could be.

There were moments when I doubted myself, questioning whether this book was worth writing. In those moments, Shelley stood by me, encouraging me to push forward and reminding me of the value in my story and perspective. Her strength carried me through not just the challenges of writing but also the ongoing struggles of dealing with PTSD, a burden I carry from my years of military service.

Shelley, your love, patience, and belief in me have been the light in my darkest moments. You've not only been my partner but also my greatest supporter and inspiration. You are an exceptional woman, and this book is as much yours as it is mine. Thank you for walking this path with me—I am forever grateful.

Contents

Preface ix

What You'll Achieve From the
C3P3 Leadership Framework xii

Introducing the C3P3 Leadership Framework xiv

PART 1: The Core of Leadership—C3 23

Chapter 1: Character: The Bedrock of Leadership 25

Chapter 2: Courage: Leading Through Uncertainty 53

Chapter 3: Conviction: Decisive Leadership in Action 69

PART 2: The Adaptive Leadership Model—P3 83

Chapter 4: Persist: The Discipline to Stay the Course 85

Chapter 5: Pivot: The Art of Adaptability 105

Chapter 6: Part-With: The Power of Letting Go 121

PART 3: Applying C3P3 to Leadership, Strategy, and Performance   **133**

Chapter 7: C3P3 in Action   135

Chapter 8: Practical Application of C3P3 Leadership with the GROW Model   147

Chapter 9: The C3P3 Leader   167

Work with Andrew   174

Bibliography   176

Preface

Leadership is the courage to persist through challenges, the wisdom to pivot when circumstances demand, and the strength to part with what hinders progress. It's not about authority or control—it's about embodying character, courage, and conviction to influence, inspire, and create lasting impact.

Leadership is a journey, not a destination. Over the course of my 30-year career in military service, government, aviation, and strategic consulting, I've come to learn that leadership is less about titles and positions and more about the lasting impact you create through your actions, decisions, and character.

Preface

This book, *C3P3 Leadership: A Framework for High-Impact Leadership, Strategy, and Performance*, is the culmination of these decades of experience and collaboration with some of the most accomplished leaders across industries. It presents a framework that will help you move from theory to practice to leading with impact.

The seeds of this framework were planted during my time in the Australian Army, where I served as a lieutenant colonel, a chief of staff, a unit commander, and an Army aviator. Leadership in the military is a test of character, courage, and conviction—often in the most complex and high-stakes environments. It was within this environment that I learned the value of persistence in the face of setbacks, the importance of pivoting to adapt to rapidly changing circumstances, and the necessity of parting with strategies, processes, or even people when they no longer served the mission. All of which became part of my own character, and part of the framework for leadership that this book presents.

My military career took me from commanding a helicopter organisation to serving on the front line to shaping international defence strategies with the United States Marine Corps in the Pentagon and many places in between. These experiences taught me that while leadership styles may vary, the core principles of leadership are universal. These true principles transcend industries and cultures. They form the foundation for sustainable success and meaningful impact for all leaders, regardless of whether you're in the military or in the corporate world.

> Leadership is less about titles and positions and more about the lasting impact you create through your actions, decisions, and character.

Since transitioning from military service, I have worked as a non-executive director, leadership coach, and managing director. These roles have allowed me to apply, reflect, and refine the C3P3 Framework in boardrooms, strategy sessions, and leadership development programs so it truly aligns with the corporate experience.

Throughout this process, I've had the privilege of mentoring C-suite executives, board directors, and emerging leaders across private, government, and community sectors. And I've seen firsthand how the C3P3 Framework has helped them navigate uncertainty, complexity, and ambiguity by embracing sustainable leadership principles.

Preface

What You'll Achieve From the C3P3 Leadership Framework

The C3P3 Leadership Framework is not a one-size-fits-all approach. It is a personalised, strategic pathway designed to empower leaders to move from awareness to action, ultimately fostering clarity, confidence, and measurable leadership impact.

Whether you're an established leader seeking to refine your approach, an emerging leader ready to take on greater challenges, or even a helicopter pilot leading a squadron, this book is for you. Each chapter is designed to challenge you, inspire you, and equip you with the practical tools to lead with confidence, purpose, and integrity.

> The C3P3 Framework will serve as a compass, guiding you to navigate the complexities of leadership and strategy to ultimately help you lead with clarity and impact.

Remember, leadership is not static—it's dynamic and evolving with every decision, challenge, and opportunity you face, so as a leader you need to be dynamic, flexible, and evolving as well. My hope is that the C3P3 Framework will serve as a compass, guiding you to navigate the complexities of leadership and strategy to ultimately help you lead with clarity and impact.

Together, we'll redefine what it means to lead with purpose and make a lasting difference in our organisations, communities, and the world.

Thank you for taking this journey with me.

—*Andrew Middleton*

Preface

Introducing the C3P3 Leadership Framework

CHARACTER – COURAGE – CONVICTION

C3P3 LEADERSHIP MODEL

UNDERSTAND INDIVIDUAL AND TEAM INNATE DRIVERS

GAIN CLARITY TO DEFINE LEADERSHIP AND TEAM TRAJECTORIES

STRATEGIC INSIGHTS

CRITICAL REFLECTION

OPPORTUNITY STATEMENT

DECISIVE ACTION

STRATEGY IMPLEMENTATION

TURN INSIGHTS AND REFLECTIONS INTO ACTIONS

IMPLEMENT, REVIEW, AND ADJUST

HIGH-IMAPCT INDIVIDUALS AND TEAMS

PERSIST – PIVOT – PART-WITH

The C3P3 Leadership Framework provides a dynamic and practical framework for leaders to develop their own leadership, guide emerging leaders, create high-performing teams and organisations, and respond well in challenging situations.

At the core of this framework is what I call the Opportunity

Statement. This is the central focus. Adapted from military doctrine, where we used *problem framing* to define current circumstances and establish a clear end state, this concept reframes the challenge as a possibility or even an opportunity. In military terms, we would create a *problem statement* to guide action. In corporate leadership, we shift the mindset from problem to opportunity and from reaction to intention.

Your Opportunity Statement becomes your strategic compass. It articulates where you are now, where you want to be, and why this matters. Whether you're building team cohesion, leading change, or developing your own influence, the Opportunity Statement provides focus and direction. It acts as the golden thread, connecting and aligning each stage of the C3P3 journey.

While this book doesn't explore the Opportunity Statement as a separate tool, its presence is felt throughout. Every leadership action, every insight, reflection, decision, and implementation serves to bridge the gap between the current state and your desired end state. Instead of asking 'What's wrong?', the Opportunity Statement asks, 'What could be?'

Underpinning the framework are six foundational pillars of leadership:

1. **Character**—The foundation of trust and ethical leadership
2. **Courage**—Making bold decisions in uncertainty

3. **Conviction**—Staying true to strategic vision and governance
4. **Persistence**—Overcoming setbacks and leading with resilience
5. **Pivoting**—Adapting with agility in a rapidly changing world
6. **Parting-with**—Knowing when to let go for progress

Anchored in our core leadership pillars, the four interrelated quadrants of the C3P3 Leadership Framework represent the essential steps leaders take to move from their current reality towards their desired end state.

Four Quadrants of the C3P3 Leadership Framework

1. Strategic Insights

The leadership journey begins with awareness of self, of others, and of context. This first step in the C3P3 Framework is about cultivating deep self-awareness and understanding the innate drivers that shape leadership behaviours. Whether you're assessing your own development, leading a team, or mentoring others, this stage lays the foundation for everything that follows.

Here you begin to explore your natural leadership energy, acquired skills, personality traits, and behavioural patterns to understand how they influence your leadership impact. The goal is to uncover what motivates leaders and drives their decisions so you can lead more effectively and authentically, both personally and through others.

This competency is grounded in the pillars of character, courage, and conviction, anchoring your insight in integrity, bold self-honesty, and alignment with your leadership purpose.

In decision-making, Strategic Insight means starting from a place of informed clarity. You gather facts, perspectives, and context so that your leadership actions are grounded not in assumption but in real understanding.

2. *Critical Reflection*

With insight comes the need for deep reflection. This competency is about taking a structured and honest look at where you are, both as a leader and as a team, and identifying the gaps between your current state and your desired future.

You build on your strategic insights to clarify what's working, what's missing, and what needs to evolve. That might mean recognising the gap between the leader you are today and the one you aspire to become or between the team you have and the one you want to lead. This is where intentional leadership choices begin to take shape.

Guided by the foundational pillars of character, courage, and conviction, this step is about alignment—ensuring that your leadership direction is based on integrity and vision.

In decision-making, Critical Reflection means getting to the heart of the matter—clearly understanding the issue, challenge, or opportunity and defining the true desired outcome before moving forward. It's the pause before the leap, the clarity before the action.

3. Decisive Action

This is where insight becomes movement—where clarity, reflection, and intention are transformed into bold and deliberate action. As a leader, this competency is about designing and implementing practical steps that move you and those you lead towards your desired impact.

Whether it's a small adjustment or a significant shift, decisive action requires you to act with confidence, grounded in the insights you've gained. The focus is not on perfection but progress—on taking the next right step with purpose.

The leadership pillars of persistence, pivoting, and parting-with are crucial here. They empower you to push through resistance, adapt when needed, and release what no longer serves your mission.

In a decision-making context, this is the moment of commitment. You assess your options, weigh your insights, and make the call—choosing to act, take a risk, or initiate change. This is where leadership becomes real. You're not just thinking about what to do but doing it.

4. Strategy Implementation

This final quadrant of the C3P3 Leadership Framework focuses on sustaining high-impact leadership over the long term. Leadership doesn't stop at the moment of decision—it continues through disciplined execution, ongoing reflection, and necessary adjustment.

> As a leader, your role is not only to set things in motion but to ensure they stay aligned with your broader vision and objectives.

Implementation is a continuous loop. You plan, act, evaluate, and adapt. And then you do it all again. As a leader, your role is not only to set things in motion but to ensure they stay aligned with your broader vision and objectives. That means reviewing progress, assessing impact, and making refinements that keep your strategy relevant and effective.

Preface

The principles of persistence, pivoting, and parting-with are central in this phase. They help you remain agile, accountable, and committed to growth, even as circumstances change.

In decision-making terms, this step ensures you're not just making a decision and moving on. Instead, you ask yourself, *'Did it work? What could I have done better? Do I need to follow up, change course, or double down?'* This is where true leadership maturity lives—in the discipline to follow through, the humility to learn, and the courage to adapt.

Why C3P3 Works

There are a lot of leadership frameworks in the world, some better than others. What sets C3P3 apart is its foundation in proven military strategic thinking, reimagined for modern leaders who are navigating complex environments. It shifts the focus from reactive problem-solving to proactive opportunity framing, helping leaders move from firefighting to forward-thinking.

C3P3 equips you to identify opportunities for growth, elevate team performance, and make deliberate, high-impact decisions. Whether you're leading a business, a project, or a personal transformation, the framework provides a structured, practical approach that can be used daily or relied on in times of change or uncertainty. It supports leaders in making sound decisions that align with their organisation's mission while also valuing the perspectives, contributions, and wellbeing of their people.

At its core, C3P3 is about inspiring purposeful action, building trust, and fostering an environment where individuals feel empowered, accountable, and connected to a shared goal. It's leadership that balances outcomes with culture and where mutual trust drives collective success.

When it comes to application, the C3P3 Leadership Framework is for individual leaders (both yourself and leaders within your organisations), for teams, and for organisations, as well as for guiding your decisions when you're in crisis or a time of change and for helping you navigate any other leadership challenges.

More than just a model, C3P3 is a mindset—one that helps you to become an influential leader through impact, effectiveness, and inspiration. Its strength lies in its flexibility to be used anywhere. The C3P3 Leadership Framework can be used:

- Individually, to elevate your own leadership capability.
- With teams, to align effort and energy towards shared goals.
- Across organisations, to anchor strategic direction and culture.
- In decision-making, especially during high-stakes or uncertain situations.

No matter the context, C3P3 helps you lead with influence, act with intent, and deliver results that matter.

Preface

However, though the application is wide, in this book, we'll focus on the six foundational pillars and explore how to apply the leadership framework:

Here's how we'll do it:

- **Part 1: The Core of Leadership** (Chapters 1–3)
  We begin with an internal look at your leadership through the lens of character, courage, and conviction. This is where you build the foundation for impactful leadership.

- **Part 2: Adaptive Leadership in Action** (Chapters 4–6)
  We explore how to pivot, persist, and part with old habits to lead through uncertainty and take strategic, decisive action.

- **Part 3: Putting it All Together** (Chapters 7–8)
  Here we move from theory to application, using practical examples to show how you can embed the C3P3 model in your leadership practice.

In every section, you'll be invited to explore how these principles apply not just in your role, but in your decisions, relationships, and broader impact.

Let's Get Started

Now that we understand the basics of the C3P3 Framework, let's look at how we can apply this to your own leadership journey, to take you to the high-impact leader you want to be.

PART 1

The Core of Leadership—C3

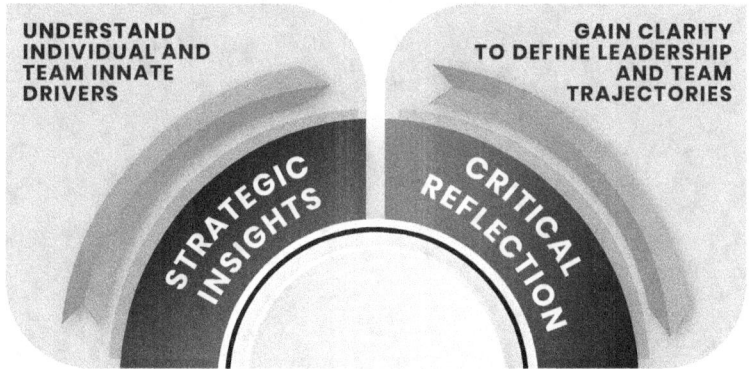

CHARACTER - COURAGE - CONVICTION

UNDERSTAND INDIVIDUAL AND TEAM INNATE DRIVERS

GAIN CLARITY TO DEFINE LEADERSHIP AND TEAM TRAJECTORIES

STRATEGIC INSIGHTS

CRITICAL REFLECTION

The C3P3 leadership journey begins with understanding who you are. This means knowing how your energy, skills, personality traits, and even behavioural tendencies work together to shape who you are as a leader. These insights form the foundation of both the C3P3 Framework and effective leadership more broadly.

The journey is anchored in character, courage, and conviction, three essential elements for developing strategic insight. And these are the elements that we'll be covering in the first part of this book. Let's get started.

- Character is about knowing who you are at your core—your values, personality, instincts, and behavioural patterns.
- Courage is the willingness to confront uncomfortable truths, challenge assumptions (including your own), and embrace vulnerability as a source of strength.
- Conviction reflects your commitment to personal growth through honest reflection, learning from assessment tools and feedback, and continually striving to be the best version of yourself.

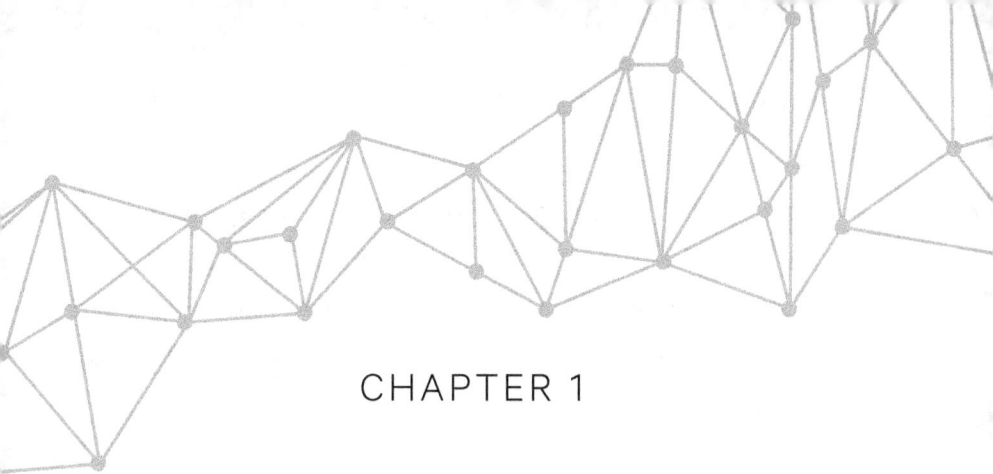

CHAPTER 1

Character: The Bedrock of Leadership

The Decoy Mission: A Test of Leadership

During a deployment to Afghanistan, I had the opportunity to work closely with British, Dutch and US helicopter forces. It was a reunion of sorts, as I had previously served with the United Kingdom's 847 Naval Air Squadron in 2003. Reconnecting with old colleagues in a war zone brought a sense of familiarity amidst the chaos.

At the time, we were running daily helicopter operations in Helmand Province, but a persistent and deadly threat loomed over these operations. The Taliban had acquired and positioned an anti-aircraft artillery (AAA) weapon in the region—likely a ZPU-2 or ZPU-4. This type of weapon consisted of Soviet-era

PART 1: The Core of Leadership—C3

14.5mm heavy machine guns mounted on a towed chassis or vehicle. This weapon was a menace to our air assets, particularly the Boeing CH-47 Chinook helicopters that were critical for resupply and troop movements because it was easy to move and extremely effective.

The Taliban also employed a deadly strategy in using the weapon. They'd keep the weapon hidden until they heard the rotors of an approaching helicopter. Once within range, the gunners would rapidly deploy the guns, fire upon the aircraft, and disappear before our side could muster any sort of counterattack.

The ongoing attacks had forced our aviation operations into a defensive posture, and this meant that our ability to support our ground forces was limited. Something had to be done.

A briefing was called at Kandahar Airfield, led by a senior aviation officer, a leader known for his boldness and tactical acumen. At the briefing, he presented a radical plan to eliminate the threat once and for all.

His idea was simple in concept but extraordinarily risky in execution. He proposed using a CH-47 Chinook as bait. The plan called for flying a Chinook deliberately low and slow through the area where the Taliban weapon had been reported. The goal was to lure the enemy into revealing their position by opening fire. The plan was risky because the Chinook, a tandem-rotor, heavy-lift transport helicopter, was one of the most valuable assets in our arsenal but also one of the most vulnerable. It was large, slow, and lightly armed, which made it an easy target for anti-aircraft fire.

The second part of the plan, and what the Taliban wouldn't know, is that we would also have an AH-64 Apache attack helicopter loitering high above in a concealed standoff position, out of sight and beyond earshot. The Apache, one of the most advanced and lethal attack helicopters in the world, was to be armed with AGM-114 Hellfire missiles, 70mm rockets, and a 30mm chain gun. The moment the Taliban-controlled anti-aircraft weapon exposed itself, the Apache would strike with pinpoint precision, destroying the threat before it could fire on the Chinook.

It was a gamble for sure, but a calculated gamble. The success of the plan relied entirely on timing—if the Taliban gunners were fast enough, they could fire on the Chinook before the Apache had a chance to neutralise them. If the Apache was faster, we had a chance to take out a weapon that had been hampering our ability to support our troops for too long. The margin for error was razor-thin, and the potential cost was catastrophic.

Recognising the immense risk, the officer made a declaration that underscored his character and leadership—he would personally fly the mission. He believed that if someone was going to fly into harm's way, it should be and would be him. He would not order any of his pilots to undertake such a dangerous task.

However, the Chinook required a co-pilot, and for this, he asked for a volunteer.

In an instant, every single pilot in the room raised their hand.

The weight of that moment was profound. It was a testament to the spirit of those who serve—men and women who understood the risks but refused to let their commander face them alone. It was also an affirmation of the leadership, trust, and deep bonds that the squadron had for this officer and each other.

> Character is your suite of individual mental and moral qualities that make up the kind of person that you are.

That day, character and courage were not just concepts—they were choices made by every pilot in that room. And it was a moment that I will never forget.

At the Heart of Every Great Leader Lies Character

That day in Afghanistan, we were shown the character that lies at the heart of a great leader. But having strong character isn't just required for military leaders—it's vital for all leaders.

Character for all of us is your suite of individual mental and moral qualities that make up the kind of person that you are. And character is the foundation of leadership.

Character defines the way that others see us, our intentions, decisions, and actions. Without strong character, no leader can command trust, and without trust, leadership is merely a title. It simply can't deliver true influence.

Character can include a wide range of different qualities and traits. However, when it comes to character traits for leaders, there are four that are hugely important. These are:

1. Integrity
2. Empathy
3. Self-Awareness
4. Resilience

Four Important Character Traits for Leadership

RESILIENCE
- Embraces Change – Adapting to new situations with flexibility.
- Demonstrates Grit – Persisting in the face of hardship
- Inspires Confidence – Encouraging others to remain optimistic and solution-focused.

INTEGRITY
- Authenticity – Being genuine and transparent.
- Accountability – Taking responsibility for decisions and actions.
  - Consistency – Following through on promises and commitments.

TRUSTED LEADERSHIP

SELF-AWARENESS
- Practices Reflection – Continuously assesses personal actions and decisions.
- Seeks Feedback – Welcomes input to improve leadership effectiveness.
- Manages Ego – Balances confidence with humility.

EMPATHY
- Listens Actively – Paying attention without judgment.
- Shows Compassion – Recognising struggles and providing support.
- Adapts Leadership Approach – Understanding individual motivations and needs.

CHARACTER-BASED

1. The Role of Integrity and Trust in Leadership

When it comes to your own leadership, the most important character trait is integrity. This is an unshakable commitment to doing what's right.

Integrity in leadership means consistency between what a leader says and what they do. Leaders with integrity align their words with their actions, creating reliability and credibility within their team, both upwards and downwards. And this in turn builds trust.

Trust is the real currency of leadership. It's what binds people together, motivating them to follow your lead and make the changes you're looking for. Research shows that trust allows your team to make assumptions about how you (as the leader) will behave in the future—and that means they have more surety about the outcomes of their own behaviour leading to more effective cooperation overall.[1]

Trust is the real currency of leadership.

Trust must be earned, however, and it's earned through a leader's integrity—that is consistent transparent behaviour, honesty and ethical decisions.

---

[1] Chen, H & Lin, Y. (July 2018). 'Goal orientations, leader-leader exchange, trust, and the outcomes of project performance.' *International Journal of Project Management.* https://www.sciencedirect.com/science/article/abs/pii/S0263786317303174.

Consider leaders like Nelson Mandela and Abraham Lincoln. Mandela, South Africa's first black president, is well known for dedicating his life to dismantling decades of white supremacist apartheid rule. Lincoln is also known for his efforts to abolish slavery, as well as preserving the Union within the United States. These leaders demonstrated integrity and an unwavering ethical stance during times of incredible adversity. The result of their strong and trustworthy leadership shaped not only their legacy but also the course of history.

Trust, once built, is extremely powerful. It's one of the most vital forms of capital that you have as a leader today. When you are a trusted leader, it creates a culture where teams feel safe and empowered to be transparent, take risks, and push boundaries in the pursuit of shared goals. Tasks get accomplished more easily, people are more likely to collaborate, communication is more productive, and outcomes are more successful.[2] But there cannot be trust without integrity.

2. The Role of Empathy in Leadership

Understanding and connecting with others on an emotional level is another core leadership character trait. We've all experienced empathy and have a sense of what it is. But by definition, empathy

---

[2] Lewis, A. (26 October 2022). 'Good Leadership? It All Starts With Trust.' Harvard Business Publishing. https://www.harvardbusiness.org/good-leadership-it-all-starts-with-trust/.

is the ability to recognise, understand, and, most importantly, share the feelings of others.

As a leader, this is important because it creates meaningful connections between you and those you are leading. And meaningful connections foster trust. It is *not* about being overly emotional, making decisions based purely on 'feelings,' or sharing every thought and emotion you, or your team, might be having. Instead, it's about being able to truly listen to the perspectives of others, creating communications that allow you to understand the challenges they're facing, and acknowledging struggles and wins as well.

This is emotional intelligence (EI), and it is enhanced by the character of empathy. In fact, leaders with high levels of empathy often have higher EI since this is one of the five main components of EI (along with self-awareness, self-regulation, internal motivation, and social skills).[3]

Emotional intelligence allows you as a leader to understand and manage your own and others' emotions, and it makes you more effective at managing relationships and guiding your team to success.

Ginni Rometty's memoir, *Good Power: Leading Positive Change*

---

[3] Cavaness, K, Picchioni, A, & Fleshman, JW. (3 June 2020). 'Linking Emotional Intelligence to Successful Health Care Leadership: The Big Five Model of Personality.' *Clinics in Colon and Rectal Surgery*. https://pmc.ncbi.nlm.nih.gov/articles/PMC7329378/.

in Our Lives, Work, and World, delves into her journey from humble beginnings to becoming IBM's first female CEO. The book emphasises the concept of 'good power,' which Rometty defines as using one's influence to serve others and drive positive change.[4]

One fantastic example of Rometty's application of emotional intelligence is her advocacy for the Skills First initiative. She recognised that traditional hiring practices often overlooked capable individuals who didn't have formal degrees but were otherwise very well suited to the role. Instead, she championed a skills-based approach—that is, looking at what the person can do, rather than just at their education.

The Skills First Initiative not only addressed business needs by helping IBM find skilled workers but also promoted inclusivity by valuing diverse backgrounds and experiences.

Throughout her tenure at IBM, Rometty adopted many initiatives that demonstrated a collaborative leadership style while also fostering open communication and valuing diverse perspectives. Her empathetic leadership approach not only enhanced team dynamics but also led to innovative solutions and organisational

---

[4] Rometty, G. (2023). *Good Power: Leading Positive Change in Our Lives, Work, and World*. Harvard Business Review Press.

growth at IBM, showcasing the importance of emotional intelligence in leadership.[5]

> Empathy becomes a leadership superpower, fostering an environment of psychological safety.

Empathy, as one of your characteristics, becomes a leadership superpower, fostering an environment of psychological safety. When you are an empathetic leader, your team will feel comfortable sharing ideas with you, admitting when they've made mistakes, and taking creative leaps of innovation without the fear of judgement or recrimination. This is real leadership trust, and empathy helps get you there.

---

5 de Jong, E. (12 December 2021). 'Fractious Australia has much to learn from the kindness and purpose of New Zealand politics.' *The Guardian*. https://www.theguardian.com/commentisfree/2021/dec/12/fractious-australia-has-much-to-learn-from-the-kindness-and-purpose-of-new-zealand-politics.

3. The Role of Self-Awareness (and Continuous Improvement) in Leadership

Understanding your own strengths and weaknesses and how they impact your leadership is vital for self-improvement, and this, in turn, is vital for effective leadership.

When you are self-aware, you're able to see where you are ready to lead and where you might need some improvement. When you aren't self-aware, you will, instead, be blind to your own limitations, unable to recognise how your actions could impact your team, and resistant to making the necessary changes. So, true leadership includes being able to look inward—understanding where you are, how you lead, and where you can and should improve.

Research shows us how important self-awareness is as leaders. When we're self-aware we see ourselves more clearly, we're more confident and creative, we make better decisions, we communicate with more clarity, and we're more effective leaders with happier teams and more profitable companies.[6]

To cultivate self-awareness, we must also be ready to improve. And this means actively seeking feedback, being open to constructive criticism, and recognising that leadership is a

---

[6] Eurich, T. (5 January 2018). 'What Self-Awareness Really Is (and How to Cultivate It).' *Harvard Business Review*. https://hbr.org/2018/01/what-self-awareness-really-is-and-how-to-cultivate-it.

continuous learning process rather than a fixed state that you achieve.

Leaders who are able to prioritise continuous improvement and learning don't just better themselves. They also powerfully model this process for their teams. And this leads to a culture that is better for growth, development, and innovation for everyone.

> **Leaders who are able to prioritise continuous improvement and learning don't just better themselves. They also powerfully model this process for their teams.**

Sataya Nadella, as CEO of Microsoft, strongly represents this character trait in the corporate 'wild'. In fact, he transformed the company's culture by prioritising a 'learn-it-all' rather than 'know-it-all' mindset.[7] This embraces Carol Dweck's research around growth mindset. Dweck, a Stanford psychologist, coined the term 'growth mindset' describing it as the belief that basic abilities can be developed through dedication and hard work.[8] In other words, through continuous improvement.

Leaders who embrace self-awareness and continuous improvement create environments where growth mindsets can flourish and are celebrated. Like Nadella championed, we need to focus on learning, not knowing. And those who commit to learning and bettering themselves become the most impactful and enduring leaders.

4. The Role of Resilience in Leadership

Having the ability to bounce back from setbacks and challenges is one of the most defining character traits of a strong leader. And it is as important for you to model this for team culture as it is for you to develop personally. That's because failures, mistakes, and setbacks are going to be part of every team, and every individual on that team will experience them as well. If you aren't able to

---

[7] Berger, C. (21 May 2024). 'Sataya Nadella transformed Microsoft's culture during his decade as CEO by turning everyone into "learn-it-alls" instead of "know-it-alls".' *Fortune*. https://fortune.com/2024/05/20/satya-nadella-microsoft-culture-growth-mindset-learn-it-alls-know-it-alls/.

[8] Dweck, C. (14 January 2016). 'What Having a "Growth Mindset" Actually Means.' *Harvard Business Review*. https://hbr.org/2016/01/what-having-a-growth-mindset-actually-means.

endure these tough times, either individually or as a team, you simply won't be able to move forward and grow.

However, resilience is not about simply *enduring* tough times. What makes it a hugely valuable character trait for a leader is its ability to empower you to adapt, learn, and emerge stronger on the other side of adversity.[9]

Again, adversity is inevitable. These could be economic downturns, workplace conflicts, or even rapid market changes—all of which might test your leadership capacity. But leaders who cultivate the character trait of resilience won't just survive these challenges—they'll be able to use them as stepping stones for growth and innovation.

Leaders who cultivate the character trait of resilience won't just survive these challenges—they'll be able to use them as stepping stones for growth and innovation.

---

[9] Sutton, J. (3 January 2019). 'What Is Resilience & Why Is It Important to Bounce Back?' *Positive Psychology*. https://positivepsychology.com/what-is-resilience/.

In *The Ride of a Lifetime*, Robert Iger shares his story as CEO of The Walt Disney Company, where he is known as being an exemplary leader who contributed to the resilience of the leadership team overall.[10] One notable example of Iger's leadership resilience is his handling of the acquisition of Pixar Animation Studios in 2006.

At the time, Disney's animation department was struggling. Though the two studios had collaborated previously (the film *Toy Story* being an excellent example), by the time of the acquisition the relationship between Disney and Pixar had deteriorated.

Iger recognised the need for change. It was his leadership resilience that enabled him to rebuild trust with Pixar's leadership, particularly Steve Jobs, and ultimately negotiate the $7.4 billion acquisition.

This turned out to be an excellent move for both studios. It revitalised Disney's animation division and led to a series of successful films. It also underscored Iger's ability to navigate challenges and drive positive outcomes as a leader.

Throughout his tenure, Iger emphasised the importance of optimism, courage, decisiveness, and fairness—qualities that not only defined his leadership style, but also fostered a culture of resilience within Disney.

---

10   Iger, R. (2019). *The Ride of a Lifetime: Lessons in Creative Leadership from 15 Years as CEO of Walt Disney Company*. Random House.

Your Character Builds Your Reputation

Your character traits work together to create a picture of your leadership, and that picture is your reputation. Your reputation is the general belief or opinion that others have of you. And as a leader, your reputation is important because it directly impacts your credibility, trust, and ability to influence others.

Your reputation as a leader acts as a safeguard against external criticism. When challenges arise, a leader's reputation for integrity and fairness often provides a buffer against the weight of potential setbacks. Your reputation isn't just important for external stakeholders—it also impacts the internal dynamics of your team. A leader with a solid reputation creates an environment where others feel motivated to maintain high standards, knowing that their contributions are aligned with the overarching vision.

But your reputation as a leader isn't built overnight. It's forged over many years, through many hard decisions, tough challenges, and moments of personal sacrifice. It's earned by demonstrating an unwavering commitment to shared values, even when it's inconvenient or unpopular.

Leaders like Steve Jobs are an excellent example of an incredible leadership reputation. Jobs was known for his visionary thinking and ability to inspire, as well as his exacting standards and sometimes ruthless leadership. Over his years at Apple he built a reputation that transcended the confines of his company and permeated the entire tech industry.

However, reputation is fragile. It takes years to build and seconds to destroy. Once lost, it's incredibly difficult to regain. Consider Adam Neumann's leadership of WeWork, which exemplifies how a leader's reputation, once tarnished, is exceedingly difficult to restore. His egotistical decision-making, characterised by extravagant spending and poor corporate governance, culminated in the company's failed Initial public offering in 2019. This debacle not only led to a dramatic decline in WeWork's valuation but also resulted in Neumann's ousting as CEO.[11]

The erosion of trust among investors and employees alike serves as a cautionary tale—a leader's reputation, painstakingly built over time, can be swiftly dismantled by unchecked ego and imprudent choices. Leaders must guard their reputation fiercely, always acting in ways that are aligned with the values they espouse. This puts them in a position to inspire confidence, respect, and admiration.

How Character Builds Resilient Teams and Organisations

Resilient teams are our goal as leaders. Because just like a resilient individual, a resilient team is better at navigating challenges,

---

11   Aran, Y & Pollman, E. (3 November 2023). 'Ousted.' *Theoretical Inquiries in Law.* https://papers.ssrn.com/sol3/papers.cfm?abstract_id=4625990.

adapting to change, and maintaining high performance. And this is what will ultimately lead to greater and sustained success.[12]

> # A team's resilience is often a reflection of the character of its leader.

A team's resilience is often a reflection of the character of its leader. Leaders with strong characters don't just dictate—they inspire. When a team faces adversity, and they will, the strength of their leader's character can go a long way to rallying the team and keeping them focused on the shared mission.

Leading Through Loss—A Testament to Character

During the war in Afghanistan, I faced one of the most challenging moments of my career—the loss of an incredible pilot, Marcus. This was a tragedy that impacted so many—his family, our

---

[12] Garrido-Moreno, A, Martín-Rojas, R & García-Morales, V. (August 2024). 'The key role of innovation and organizational resilience in improving business performance: A mixed-methods approach.' *International Journal of Information Management.* https://www.sciencedirect.com/science/article/pii/S0268401224000252.

PART 1: The Core of Leadership—C3

squadron, and even the community. It was also an event that tested my leadership, my character, and the trust my team placed in me.

The loss of Marcus during operations was an absolutely devastating blow to our unit of young, inexperienced pilots who were already navigating the harsh realities of combat in an unfriendly country.

Marcus was more than a colleague to all of us. He was the kind of person everyone gravitated towards. We referred to him as an exceptional 'hands and feet' pilot, one who could make a helicopter dance in the skies. He was a valued and beloved member of our team, and his loss sent shockwaves through our tight-knit group.

After repatriating Marcus to his family and attending his full military funeral—complete with a flypast by our squadron—we returned to operations. But the transition was anything but easy. Marcus's loss plunged our morale and motivation to their lowest point ever.

The grief was palpable, and worries lingered in the minds of our squadron as well as those outside of our unit. But as their leader, I knew that giving in to fear or hesitation would not honour our mission or the tragic loss of our friend and colleague.

However, some of my colleagues within the aviation corps

Chapter 1: Character: The Bedrock of Leadership

suggested that I might be pushing my team too hard. They felt that I could possibly be risking another tragedy.

Yet, I knew that my role as the squadron commander was to steady the ship and rebuild trust, confidence, and focus within my squadron. So we continued to fly missions and undertake operations while I did everything in my power to support my officers and soldiers. Over the course of many months, I listened to their concerns, addressed their needs, and created space for their grief. However, I also understood that getting through this complex and emotionally charged time would come down, in a great deal, to the trust the team had in me.

In front of my unit, I remained strong and led by example. I worked long hours to make sure that every detail of each of our operations was meticulously planned and executed to minimise any risk while still achieving the mission objectives. I began to fly missions alongside the squadron to show that I wasn't asking them to do anything I wasn't willing to do myself. And I continued to listen and create space for everyone's grief.

One evening, after briefing the team for the next day's mission, one of my pilots stayed behind. He approached me quietly and said, 'Sir, you've done everything to look after us and keep us focused on the mission. But who's looking after you?' That moment hit me like a lightning bolt. Leadership can indeed be lonely, and in that instance, I realised just how much I was shouldering alone. It was a moment of self-awareness.

PART 1: The Core of Leadership—C3

Despite the emotional weight, I fell back on my foundations, the values and beliefs that had shaped me over my career in uniform. In the quiet moments between tasks, I used what little time I had to reflect. I recognised that I was carrying the burden of the squadron largely on my own, but I also understood that waiting for someone else to step in wasn't an option. Through quiet self-talk, I reminded myself that I had the strength to lead, but I also needed to acknowledge the toll it was taking.

I thought a lot about Marcus and the kind of man he was and what he would expect of us in the face of adversity. I knew he would want the team to keep going, to find strength in one another, and to honour him through action. So I made a deliberate choice—to lead with purpose, to be the anchor my team needed amid the uncertainty. Even when I was running on empty, I showed up. I kept us moving. And I led with steadiness and heart—not because it was easy, but because that's what my squadron needed, and it's what Marcus would have done.

Ultimately, it was those same character traits that gave my squadron faith in me and allowed us to rebuild morale, refocus on our mission, and honour the legacy of our fallen comrade. They knew that I would never ask them to do anything I wouldn't do myself. They trusted that they could share their feelings and worries openly, and they knew that I was doing my utmost to keep everyone safe. Trust and integrity were the invisible threads that bound us together during that difficult time, enabling us to push forward as a cohesive unit.

This experience underscored a fundamental truth about leadership that applies whether you're a squadron leader in the military or a c-suite leader in the corporate environment—namely that character is the foundation upon which everything else is built in leadership.

> Character is the foundation upon which everything else is built in leadership.

Character is what enables leaders to make tough and often unpopular decisions, navigate adversity, and inspire others to follow. Without it, leadership crumbles under the weight of doubt and mistrust, flounders in the face of adversity, and simply can't make an impact or drive influence.

For me, this chapter of my life remains a testament to the unshakable power of character. It reinforced that integrity, empathy, self-awareness, and resilience are not just ideals—they are what is needed to earn trust and lead.

> Character is what enables leaders to make tough and often unpopular decisions, navigate adversity, and inspire others to follow.

Takeaways

Character is not merely a quality—it's the very essence of leadership. Without character, leadership lacks foundation, and without trust, a leader's influence is limited. A leader who upholds their character through difficult decisions, maintains consistency in their actions, and creates an environment where teams are not only resilient but also motivated to strive for excellence.

As we move through the framework of leadership in this book, remember that it is the strength of your character that will serve as the anchor in turbulent times and the catalyst for your teams' long-term success.

🎯 Call to Action

Leadership begins with character, and character begins with you. As you reflect on the principles in this chapter, ask yourself:

- Are your words and actions aligned?
- Do you inspire trust through integrity and consistency?
- Do you build a culture of empathy and psychological safety?
- Are you focused on understanding your own strengths and weaknesses and improving where you see gaps?
- How are you building and safeguarding your reputation as a leader?

Character is the first 'C' in the C3P3 framework and the foundation for the rest of the framework and book. If you're ready to develop your leadership foundation, start by committing to building a legacy rooted in character, and you'll be on your way.

Let this be your moment to lead with purpose, navigate adversity with integrity, and create teams that thrive through trust. The path starts here. Are you ready to lead?

Tools: Using Profile Assessments to Deepen Self-Awareness and Strengthen Your Character

Character-driven leadership must include self-awareness—an honest, internal reflection on your values, motivations, and behavioural tendencies. To truly understand your character and innate drivers, it's essential to examine not only how you see yourself but also how others—subordinates, peers, and superiors—perceive you. External feedback serves as a mirror, revealing insights that may be difficult to recognise on your own.

One of the most effective ways to gain this perspective is through 360-degree feedback, a structured method that gathers confidential input from those who interact with you regularly. This feedback provides a holistic view of your leadership style, strengths, and areas that may require development. When combined with self-reflection, it becomes a powerful tool for personal growth.

However, the real value of 360-degree feedback comes when it is paired with intentional reflection and action planning. By comparing external feedback with your own self-assessment, you can identify gaps between your intentions and their real-world impact. This process not only sharpens your self-awareness, but also enables you to make conscious adjustments to better align your leadership with principles of integrity, trust, and reputation.

Incorporating 360-degree feedback into your leadership journey signals a commitment to continuous improvement. It fosters trust among those you lead, reinforcing the idea that character is not just an abstract ideal but a lived practice—one that evolves through reflection, feedback, and deliberate action.

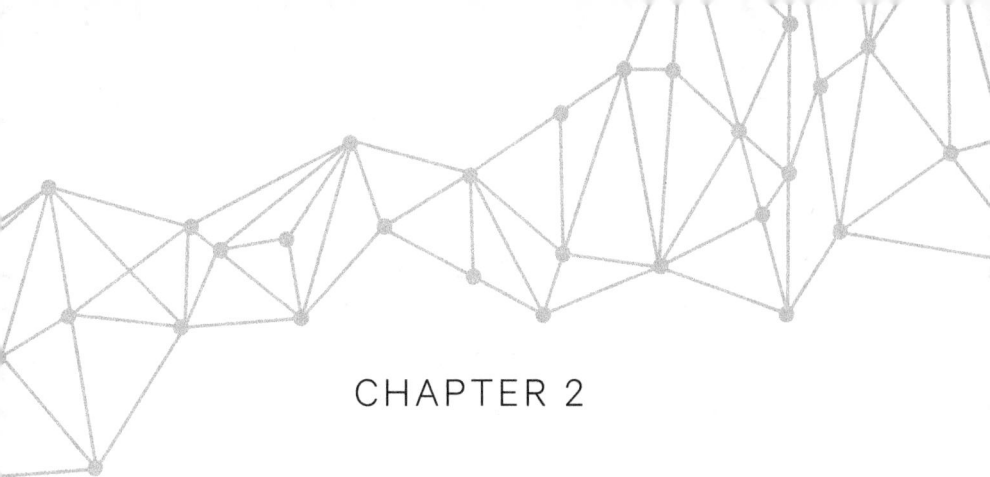

CHAPTER 2

Courage: Leading Through Uncertainty

Decision-Making Under Pressure

In leadership, the ability to make decisions quickly and decisively, especially under pressure, is one of the most vital skills a leader can possess.

During a deployment to Afghanistan, the general commanding our region of responsibility frequently flew into remote regions to conduct *shuras*—traditional Afghan council meetings held with local village elders and tribal leaders. These gatherings were a vital part of our counterinsurgency strategy, helping to build relationships, earn trust, and foster local support in areas plagued by Taliban influence.

On one such day, while the general was engaged in a *shura*, word came through that a British outpost in Kajaki Dam was under sustained attack. The fighting was intense—they were firing up to 600 mortar rounds a day just to hold their position. Critically low on ammunition, they requested an emergency resupply. Without it, they risked being overrun.

The only helicopters in the vicinity capable of carrying out the resupply were those assigned to the general's detail. I had minutes—maybe less—to make a decision. Despite the risks and the fact that the aircraft were supporting a senior leader in an unsecured environment, I made the call—re-task the Chinooks, under Apache escort, to deliver the ammunition.

While not ideal, the general had substantial ground security in place, and a UAV was providing overhead surveillance throughout the meeting. The helicopters completed the mission to Kajaki Dam and returned safely to extract the general after the resupply.

Upon their return to headquarters, the chief of staff—who had been accompanying the general—stormed into the Tactical Operations Centre and demanded I report to the general immediately. He was livid, accusing me of overstepping and making a reckless decision by diverting the aircraft. The weight of his words, combined with the gravity of the decision I had just made, hit hard. I felt the knot tighten in my stomach as I walked into the room where the general was waiting, the chief of staff looming behind me.

I stood to attention and explained the situation—what was happening in Kajaki Dam, the urgency of the resupply, and the reasons behind my decision.

The general listened quietly. Then, without hesitation, he looked me in the eye and said, 'Good call.'

That was it. No fanfare, no lecture—just calm, confident validation from a commander who understood the bigger picture. Kajaki Dam had to be held. Prioritising the men on the ground was the right thing to do.

As I turned to leave the room, I glanced at the chief of staff, stood tall, and walked out with my head high. I had been under immense pressure, but I had weighed the risks and made a decision. It was the right decision—and one I remain proud of to this day.

Making Courageous Decisions

The landscape in which you will operate as a leader is rarely static. Markets change, teams evolve, and crises emerge often without warning. So what separates great leaders from the rest is their capacity to make sound and efficient decisions in the face of uncertainty, fear, and complexity.

Courage is the linchpin that enables leaders to move forward when the path is unclear. It's the thing that allows you to face that uncertainty, fear, and complexity and continue to lead and even lead well. Courage allows you to recognise that while your decisions might carry risk, your indecision and delay can be even more costly. Great leaders can sift through the noise, identify core issues, and act. Whether it's by launching a new initiative to respond to market changes, making a tough call in a team crisis, or even admitting that you've made a mistake in managing change. When you are a courageous decision-maker, you will build trust and keep your team aligned with a common purpose.

The ability to act with clarity, even when the outcome is uncertain, is a mark of true leadership. In *Road to Power: How GM's Mary Barra Shattered the Glass Ceiling*, Laura Colby chronicles the remarkable ascent of Mary Barra, culminating in her appointment as the first female CEO of General Motors (GM).[13]

In her book, Colby focuses on a defining moment that occurred during the 2014 ignition switch crisis that showcased Barra's courage in leadership. At that time, Barra discovered that GM had delayed recalling vehicles with faulty ignition switches even though the defect had already been linked to multiple fatalities. This was a serious problem. But instead of deflecting, Barra confronted the issue head-on.

Demonstrating transparency and accountability, she ordered a comprehensive internal investigation and openly testified before Congress, acknowledging the company's failures and committing

---

13   Colby, L. (2015). *Road to Power: How GM's Mary Barra Shattered the Glass Ceiling.* Wiley.

to systemic changes going forward. She was quick and decisive, and her response not only addressed the immediate safety concerns, but also initiated a cultural transformation within GM, one that emphasised integrity and responsiveness across the board.

Barra's actions during this crisis exemplify courageous leadership, as she navigated the company through intense scrutiny while steadfastly prioritising customer safety and corporate responsibility.

Though we often think of courage as being able to confront scary situations—and of course, this is often the case—courage doesn't mean acting recklessly. Instead, as a leader, courage means gathering the necessary information, weighing the risks, and taking the first step towards a solution, regardless of the challenges.

The Link Between Courage and Effective Risk-Taking

Even though courageous leadership doesn't mean acting recklessly, it does often involve taking risks. Risks generally can either propel an organisation to new heights, if they're the right risks, or threaten its survival, if they're not. Courageous leaders understand that calculated, thoughtful risk-taking is vital to growth and innovation.

Think of Elon Musk's journey with SpaceX. The idea of privately funding a spacecraft company was, at the time, seen as incredibly risky. Musk faced numerous setbacks, including multiple failed launches. But he had the courage to continue, learn from mistakes, and refine his approach, which, ultimately, revolutionised the space industry.[14]

Like Musk, we see that the ability to take smart, calculated risks can create breakthrough opportunities that competitors may not even be in a position to see. However, the opposite is also true. Leaders who shy away from taking risks for fear of failure can miss opportunities for innovation and growth, which can lead the organisation to stagnate.

Many leaders are naturally risk averse, particularly in highly regulated fields like banking or mining. As leaders, however, it's essential to distinguish between risk aversion and risk tolerance. While a risk-averse leader might focus on protecting the status quo, a risk-tolerant leader is focused on innovation, even if it means stepping into the unknown. And while we can't avoid all risk (and shouldn't aim to), we can operate within our own risk tolerances. The key is balancing bold moves with sound judgement, ensuring that risks are taken strategically to further the organisation's vision.

---

14 Howell, E. (27 April 2022). 'SpaceX: Facts about Elon Musk's private spaceflight company.' Space.com. https://www.space.com/18853-spacex.html.

Courage in Leadership—Navigating Uncertainty

Courage is tested in the toughest of times, and often the most challenging decisions are made during crises. While military leaders are regularly faced with decisions that involve life or death, corporate leaders will face decisions that can make or break a team or organisation, and in all cases they must act decisively, sometimes even when they lack complete information or time to consider it fully. Being able to remain composed and lead through high-stress situations takes courage.

One of the moments that most tested my courage and resolve during my leadership journey occurred when I inherited an underperforming and frankly disruptive team leader within my unit. They had already been moved from department to department before arriving under my command. Despite their history, I approached them with an open mind, wanting to give them the benefit of the doubt and have a real opportunity to excel.

It quickly became apparent, however, that this individual was in a rank and position beyond their ability. Their performance consistently fell below standard, and their behaviour created significant disruptions within my unit and external organisations. This then jeopardised the morale of our team and the reputation of the unit.

Despite these challenges, I decided I wouldn't just ignore the problem or simply move them along to another department, as had been done previously. Instead, I committed to mentoring and coaching them. I was determined to help them grow into their role.

Unfortunately, despite my best efforts, their conduct continued to negatively impact the team and the unit. After numerous counselling sessions and documented interventions, I made the difficult decision to report on their lack of suitability for continued service. This was a hard decision, and it wasn't without consequences. The individual lodged a complaint against me, which led to an investigation into my leadership.

This was a hugely challenging time—one where I faced immense personal and professional pressure. I had to maintain my composure, continue performing my duties at a high level, and lead my team while experiencing uncertainties from the investigation. There was risk to my reputation and I had to have courage to maintain my confidence as a leader while this was all going on in the background. Yet I stood firm. I knew that addressing the issue was the right thing to do for both the individual and the unit and even for my leadership.

I was cleared from the claims. After this, some of the individuals' previous supervisors reached out to commend me for my courage and integrity. They acknowledged that I had done what they—and many others—had avoided. This experience reinforced for me that true leadership requires the courage to make tough decisions, even when it might be easier (personally or professionally or both) to look the other way.

Practical Steps to Cultivate Courage in Leadership Roles

While some leaders may appear naturally courageous, courage in leadership is a skill that can be developed over time. However, cultivating courage in leadership isn't always easy. It involves both mental fortitude and emotional intelligence, and it naturally involves facing challenging circumstances (you can't have courage without challenge).

Below are practical steps leaders can take to foster courage in themselves and within their teams:

Step 1: Lead by Example

Demonstrate courage in your own actions. When you face challenges, be transparent with your team about the risks, the opportunities, and the reasoning behind your decisions. Then make your decision and take action. Your openness and vulnerability, along with your willingness to stand firm in your decision-making, will encourage others to do the same.

Step 2: Embrace Failure as a Learning Opportunity

Fear of failure often holds leaders back from making bold decisions. But failure is an inevitable part of growth. Instead of seeing failure as just that—failure—try to adopt a mindset shift, one where failure is seen as a stepping stone to learning and improvement, rather than a setback to be feared and avoided.

Step 3: Build a Supportive Network

An individual's courage can often be bolstered by surrounding themselves with trusted colleagues, advisors, and peers. Sometimes even family and friends can serve this purpose. Whoever you choose, these people should be willing to challenge you, give you honest feedback, and support you through any difficult decisions. A strong support network can make taking courageous steps less daunting and help you make better and more efficient decisions.

Step 4: Stay Focused on the Big Picture

Courage often wanes when leaders lose sight of their overarching goals. Keep your vision clear and revisit it regularly. Remind yourself what you're trying to achieve and why. When you remain connected to your objectives, then it's easier to manage fears and setbacks, which might otherwise feel more overwhelming.

Step 5: Practice Self-Reflection

Self-awareness is a key component of courage, but to truly have self-awareness you need to regularly review and assess your decision-making process and reflect on how you navigated past challenges (both the good and the bad). Go over the decisions you've made that required courage, and how you navigated them. What would you do differently next time? Learning from past experiences will give you the confidence you need to take courageous actions in the future.

Step 6: Foster a Culture of Courage

As a leader, you must be courageous yourself, but it's equally important to inspire courage in your team. This can be a challenge, but you start by creating a culture where people are psychologically safe and feel supported in taking risks, speaking up, and making decisions.[15] And once people take the opportunity to step up to the plate and demonstrate courage in the workplace, be sure to recognise and celebrate those individuals and moments, even when the outcome is uncertain. This reinforces a culture of bravery and initiative and shows that it's something that you truly embrace and not just talk about.

---

15 Gallo, A. (15 February 2023). 'What Is Psychological Safety?' *Harvard Business Review.* https://hbr.org/2023/02/what-is-psychological-safety.

Takeaway

The big takeaway is to remember that courage as a leader is not about recklessness or confronting fear. And it's not just about making the right decision. It's about acting decisively and ethically, even when the consequences are uncertain or challenging for you personally or professionally, and it's about persevering through the fallout and staying aligned with the bigger picture. Courageous leaders are willing to confront discomfort, navigate uncertainty, and trust in their preparation and values to guide themselves and their team through any storm.

True leaders demonstrate courage in these times of crisis, of course. But they also demonstrate courage in the everyday decisions they take that shape the future of their organisations. When you cultivate courage as a leader, you will be in a position to make bold moves, build resilient teams, and ultimately achieve your vision—no matter the obstacles that lay in your path.

>  **Call to Action**
>
> As you move forward in your leadership journey, take a moment to reflect on the courage it takes to lead through uncertainty.
>
> Ask yourself—how will you approach your next tough decision? Will you allow fear to hold you back, or will you take the first step towards a solution, even when the outcome is unclear? Commit to cultivating courage in yourself and your team today and watch how it transforms your leadership.

Tool: The Courage Compass

The Courage Compass is a practical tool designed to help leaders develop and practice courage in decision-making and risk-taking. This tool combines self-awareness, reflection, and actionable strategies to guide leaders to become more courageous both in their everyday activities and in the face of uncertainty.

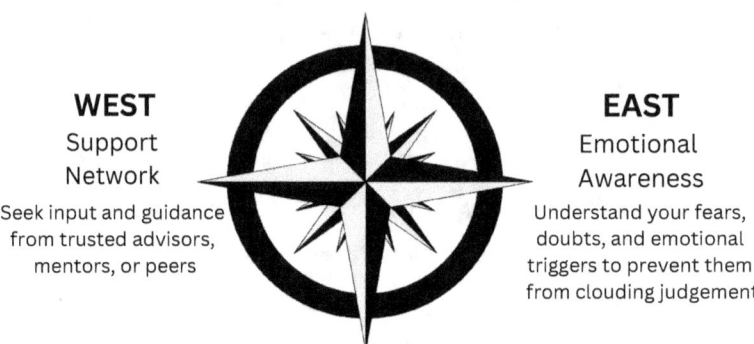

NORTH
Values Alignment
Define and stay connected to your core values and the mission of your organisation

WEST
Support Network
Seek input and guidance from trusted advisors, mentors, or peers

EAST
Emotional Awareness
Understand your fears, doubts, and emotional triggers to prevent them from clouding judgement

SOUTH
Situational Awareness
Assess the risks, gather necessary information, and determine the potential impact of your decision

How to Use the Courage Compass

Step 1: Reflect before action—*Before taking any action, particularly when facing a tough decision, pause and consider each point of the Courage Compass.*

Step 2: Take action with confidence—*Once you've gleaned insights from the Courage Compass, you will be able to make a thoughtful, courageous decision that is aligned with your values* and that has been thoughtfully considered with the support of your most trusted colleagues.

Step 3: Review and learn—*After you've taken action, review the decision and its outcomes. How did things work out? Where could improvements be made? These steps allow you to refine your courage-building skills for the future.*

The Courage Compass gives you the practical steps you need to ground your leadership actions and decisions in your values. It will ultimately help you build the courage to lead decisively and ethically, whether it's in your everyday acts or as you lead through uncertainty and crisis.

CHAPTER 3

Conviction: Decisive Leadership in Action

The Power of Leading with Purpose and Clarity

The definition of conviction is simple—'a strong opinion or belief'.[16] But having conviction in your leadership means something a little bit more. It means you have an unshakeable belief in your vision, your mission, and the values that drive every leadership decision you make, no matter the external pressures.

Jeff Bezos demonstrated leadership conviction in his leadership at Amazon. In the 1990s, when Bezos founded Amazon, it was really just an online bookstore. But Bezos recognised the opportunities to expand into new products and services. So rather than focusing on sales and revenue alone, which would

---

16 Conviction. (2025). In *Cambridge University Press & Assessment 2025.* https://dictionary.cambridge.org/dictionary/english/conviction.

lead to short-term profitability, he prioritised long-term growth based on market leadership. He reinvested profits into growth and infrastructure and kept his focus on the customer and creating user-friendly services, like Prime.

Not everyone agreed with this approach, and many critics initially questioned Jeff Bezos' strategy, wondering why he didn't look at making more profit in the short term. But Bezos stayed firm to his plan, and this focus on the future and on becoming a market leader, and his unwavering belief in the company's long-term potential led to Amazon becoming the global e-commerce powerhouse it is today.[17]

Like Bezos, conviction in your leadership makes your actions both deliberate and authentic and leads to excellent outcomes and incredible buy-in from those around you.

Leaders with strong conviction are able to stand firm in their values, decisions, and the actions they take—even in the face of adversity. They know where they're going and why, and this certainty permeates every aspect of their leadership, from setting strategy to guiding teams through difficult challenges. These are the kinds of leaders that people love to follow.

Why? Leaders with conviction—like Bezos—are inspirational to others because of their deep sense of purpose and the clarity

---

17 Stone, B. (2021). *Amazon Unbound: Jeff Bezos and the Invention of a Global Empire.* Simon & Schuster.

that they have in all their decisionmaking. When you lead with conviction, people can see that you really believe in what you're doing. And then they follow because they're able to adopt this belief themselves.

On the other hand, leaders *without* conviction can appear hesitant. Worse, they may appear to be—or even are—easily swayed by the opinions of others and prone to second-guessing their choices. This can undermine their ability to lead others.

Another good example of an inspirational leader with conviction is Apple co-founder Steve Jobs. When Jobs returned to the company in the late 1990s, Apple was on the brink of collapse. But Jobs had an unwavering conviction in the company's potential. He shared his vision for the company's future based on innovative technology, simplicity, and design, and this transformed Apple from a struggling company into one of the most valuable brands in the world.

Jobs' firm conviction not only brought Apple out of its struggles, taking it from a company that made $7 billion in revenue in 1997[18] to a company that netted $390.8 billion in 2024,[19] but it also made

---

18 Richter, F. (21 December 2016). 'Apple's Growth Since Re-Hiring Steve Jobs 20 Years Ago.' statista. https://www.statista.com/chart/7330/apple-revenue-since-1997/.
19 Curry, D. (18 February 2025). 'Apple Statistics (2025).' Business of Apps. https://www.businessofapps.com/data/apple-statistics/.

it a world-leading brand that has quite literally reshaped the tech industry.[20]

Conviction Drives Certainty and Certainty Drives Engagement

As humans, we crave certainty. Travis Bradberry, President of TalentSmart, explained our drivers for certainty at the World Economic Forum, saying, 'Our brains are so geared up for certainty that our subconscious can monitor and store over two million data points, which the brain uses to predict the future'. Two million data points! That's how much of our mind we use simply to find certainty.[21]

Like Bezos demonstrated, when you are a leader who leads with purpose and clarity, you are then able to create a strong, unified direction for your team, which leads to incredible outcomes. This is because you are able to communicate your vision so effectively that others feel compelled to follow, even when facing obstacles or challenges.

Leaders with conviction create an environment of certainty for everyone, and when a leader is certain of the path they are forging, everyone who follows them absorbs this belief as well. This is the

---

20 Isaacson, W. (2011). *Steve Jobs*. Simon & Schuster.
21 Bradberry. T. (7 December 2015). 'Why the best leaders have conviction.' World Economic Forum. https://www.weforum.org/stories/2015/12/why-the-best-leaders-have-conviction/.

power of conviction in leadership. It has the unmatched ability to align and mobilise people towards a common goal, creating a shared sense of responsibility and momentum within their team and organisation.

Strategy Through the Lens of Conviction

Conviction also plays an especially critical role in strategic decision-making as a leader, which can be a large part of your leadership requirements. Having conviction as a leader, even when making high-level decisions that might impact that entire organisation, is not about being stubborn or rigid in your thinking.

Instead, conviction is about having the courage to stand by your principles and decisions, even when you're facing opposition or uncertainty (and as a leader, you certainly will). This type of conviction allows you to push forward strategically, recognising that challenges and setbacks are often part of the process.

Your conviction ensures that you, your team, your organisation, and any other stakeholders remain committed to your overarching objectives while still being able to adapt to any changes either externally or internally that might come up. And adaptability is key to ensuring your long-term vision is achieved as a leader.

Balancing Long-Term Vision with Adaptability

One of the key challenges for leaders with conviction is balancing your long-term vision with the need for adaptability. But being adaptable while still being able to stand by your convictions is what makes a leader a great leader. In fact, research shows us that being able to find the balance between conviction and adaptability is the hallmark of high-performing leadership.[22]

Finding that balance means that as a leader you'll know when to stand firm and when to pivot. While conviction demands staying true to the mission and vision, effective leaders are flexible enough to adjust their strategy based on new information, changing circumstances, or unforeseen disruptions.

Rigid or stubborn conviction can actually hinder your ability to be adaptable and innovative and lead you to miss important opportunities. While being completely flexible can cause you—and your team—to lose your sense of direction.

It's the balance that's essential. So, to be an effective and high-performing leader, you must learn to lead while constantly reassessing the environment and remaining true to your core

---

22 McCarthy, K, O'Connell, D & Hall, D. (September 2005). 'Leading beyond tragedy: The balance of personal identity and adaptability.' *Leadership & Organization Development Journal.* https://www.researchgate.net/publication/242348015_Leading_beyond_tragedy_The_balance_of_personal_identity_and_adaptability.

values—but also adjusting tactics when necessary to remain relevant and responsive to the changing world.

A great example of leadership conviction can be found in *Alibaba: The House That Jack Ma Built*. Author Duncan Clark chronicles Jack Ma's journey from an English teacher to the founder of one of the world's largest e-commerce companies. A particularly striking moment came in 2005, when Ma accepted a $1 billion investment from Yahoo in exchange for a 40% stake in Alibaba. While this decision brought much-needed capital and global credibility, it also introduced long-term challenges around ownership and control.[23]

It was an uphill battle, but in the years that followed, Ma remained steadfast in preserving Alibaba's autonomy, eventually leading efforts to buy back Yahoo's stake. This balance between strategic partnership and long-term vision highlights Ma's commitment to Alibaba's mission and values and ultimately contributed to the company's enduring success.

Conviction in Humanitarian Leadership During the 2005 Banda Aceh Tsunami Disaster Relief

The 2004 Indian Ocean tsunami devastated large swaths of South-east Asia, including the region of Banda Aceh, Indonesia. In

---

23 Clark, D. (2016). *Alibaba: The house that Jack Ma built*. Harper Collins US.

PART 1: Conviction: Decisive Leadership in Action

fact, the scale of destruction was beyond comprehension. Entire towns were wiped out, children were ripped from parents' arms, and enormous container ships were found one kilometre inland.

The Indonesian city was in ruins, over 200,000 people were killed, and millions more were displaced. Military forces from around the world, as well as numerous non-governmental organisations (NGOs), descended on the region to provide aid, recover bodies, and offer whatever assistance they could. Amidst this chaos, the Indonesian National Armed Forces (known as the TNI) was also heavily involved, sometimes in a controversial capacity given the political dynamics of the region.

I was deployed as a captain leading a troop of UH-1H helicopters for disaster relief operations in Banda Aceh. Our mission was clear—we were to prioritise humanitarian aid by delivering supplies, assisting in recovery, and supporting the Indonesian authorities. But the chaos brought constant challenges for everyone involved—including my own leadership. These challenges ranged from external pressures from families missing loved ones and international agencies, ethical dilemmas, and even a complex operational environment.

One particular challenge that I faced was when I was approached by two non-uniformed men to personally conduct reconnaissance missions over military airfields. I was tasked with reporting on Indonesian aircraft types and numbers and monitoring military activities in the region. This request put me in a difficult position. I was in Banda Aceh for humanitarian work, not military intelligence. Indonesian Mi-24 Hind, a Soviet-designed attack helicopter with troop transport capabilities, frequently shadowed our humanitarian flights, ensuring that we were doing that work—and that work only. But there were military operations going on alongside the relief efforts, which meant a lot of tension in the region.

Despite ongoing pressure, I was determined to remain fully convicted to the core purpose of my mission and not to get involved in covert intelligence work. I also knew that flying over military airfields, under the guise of a humanitarian mission, would not only compromise my integrity and the integrity of my team but could also escalate tensions in an already politically sensitive area.

As the captain in charge of my troop, I was leading independently from the Joint Task Force headquarters in Medan. This responsibility weighed heavily on me, as the right decisions had to be made quickly. These pressures made the temptation to deviate from our core mission strong, but my own values demanded that I remain fully focused on recovery and relief efforts. I also knew that if I compromised our focus, I risked losing that trust and the integrity of our mission.

So, despite the external pressures, I stayed true to my convictions and kept our flights strictly within the parameters of providing aid, recovery, and support to the people of Banda Aceh.

The impact of this decision was twofold. First, it helped maintain the integrity of the relief operation and kept important relief efforts focused on the people in need after an incredibly terrible tragedy. Second, it helped prevent any escalation of tensions in the region. By staying firm in my convictions, I helped protect both the mission and the diplomatic sensitivities of working in a foreign country in the middle of a crisis.

Takeaways

Leading with conviction means understanding not just *what* you're doing but *why* you're doing it. It's this unwavering belief in a cause or a set of values that drives the relentless pursuit of goals that are aligned with that purpose. And it's that alignment that inspires others to follow you in your decision-making to create lasting impact.

Staying true to my mission's core objective—humanitarian aid—meant I was able to make decisive, ethical decisions, even amidst the chaos and external pressures. In the same vein, all leaders are better able to perform more effectively and lead well when they're leading with clarity and purpose. My commitment to the mission provided direction, and your conviction to your own purpose will provide direction to your own leadership as well.

It's through unwavering commitment to the 'mission' (whatever that means to your own leadership) that you'll be able to make the tough decisions that keep your strategy on track with your purpose, inspire your teams, and ultimately create a meaningful and lasting impact.

Call to Action

As you continue your leadership journey, take a moment to reflect on the power of conviction in guiding your decisions. Ask yourself:

1. How will you ensure your actions align with your core purpose, even when external pressures push you in different directions?

2. How will you stay true to your values when another purpose might be the goal of others in your organisation?

Leading with conviction is about staying steadfast in your purpose and inspiring others to follow with confidence. Your goal now is to commit to leading with clarity, purpose, and an unwavering belief in your purpose, values, and vision.

Tool: Personal Leadership Philosophy Statement

A fantastic tool for helping you to lead with conviction is to create a written commitment that defines your leadership purpose and values. This Personal Leadership Philosophy Statement can then serve as a guiding principle for making leadership decisions and staying accountable.

How to Create a Personal Leadership Philosophy Statement:

1. **Define your core values**—The first step is to identify three to five principles or values that guide your leadership (e.g., integrity, accountability, or service).

2. **Clarify your leadership purpose**—Once you've identified your guiding principles, write a one-sentence mission statement about why you lead. This should implement your core values.

3. **Commit to non-negotiables**—Now that you have your leadership purpose, list the actions and behaviours you will never compromise on that will help you achieve that purpose.

4. **Establish decision-making guidelines**—Now write a simple framework that will help you evaluate tough choices based on your core values and your purpose.

This should include a final question where you ask yourself, 'Does this decision align with my values?'

5. **Review and reflect regularly**—Your last step is to commit to a quarterly reflection on how you're aligning your leadership with your convictions. When you aren't quite marrying them up, what changes can you make to do this better?

Examples of Personal Leadership Philosophy Statements

Personal Leadership Philosophy Statement—Corporate Executive

As a corporate executive, I lead with integrity, adaptability, and respect. My purpose is to empower high-performing teams to deliver sustainable value while fostering a culture of trust and innovation. I am committed to ethical leadership, transparent communication, and accountability—these are non-negotiables in how I lead and the behaviours I expect from those around me.

When faced with complex decisions, I will ask: *Does this course of action align with our company values? Does it serve our people, clients, and long-term strategy?* I will regularly reflect on my actions and decisions to ensure they are consistent with this philosophy and adjust my approach when needed. Through clarity, consistency, and compassion, I will lead with purpose and create meaningful impact across the business.

Personal Leadership Philosophy Statement—Project Lead

As a project lead, I value clarity, adaptability, and ownership. My purpose is to bring people together with a shared vision, ensuring we deliver outcomes that are efficient, effective, and aligned with our strategic objectives. I see leadership as the art of coordination—ensuring the right people, processes, and resources are in place to succeed.

I will never compromise on transparency, follow-through, or mutual respect. I hold myself and others accountable to timelines, standards, and respectful collaboration.

When making decisions, I ask: *Does this support the project's success? Are we solving the right problem? Is it fair, timely, and well-communicated?* I commit to reviewing my leadership approach regularly and making adjustments where needed. I lead with the mindset that progress is built through teamwork, trust, and clear direction.

PART 2

The Adaptive Leadership Model—P3

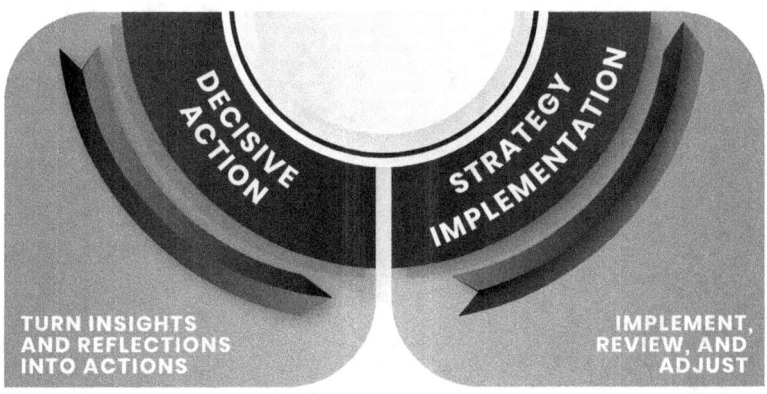

In this second part of the C3P3 Leadership Framework we move on to the next three foundational pillars. These are persistence, or overcoming setbacks and leading with resilience, pivoting, or adapting with agility in a rapidly changing world, and parting-with, or knowing when to let go for progress.

Combined with the three Cs, these pillars are the building blocks of high-impact leadership. Taken together, they offer you, as a leader, a blueprint for making a difference that lasts.

Let's get started.

CHAPTER 4

Persist: The Discipline to Stay the Course

Persistence vs. Stubbornness

Henry Ward Beecher, a famous American rhetorician, said, 'The difference between perseverance and obstinacy is that one often comes from a strong will, and the other from a strong won't.'

In leadership, persistence is often celebrated as a crucial trait. But it's important to distinguish persistence from mere stubbornness or obstinacy. One is vital for helping you to achieve your goals—whether individually or as a leader. The other is a recipe for failure.

So what's the real difference in terms of leadership?

Persistence is when you keep trying until you find the way to achieve your goal. The leader who persists is willing to keep

PART 2: The Adaptive Leadership Model—P3

moving forward, even when faced with adversity, but they are also smart enough to recognise when the path needs to shift. Stubbornness, on the other hand, can manifest as a refusal to change or adapt, even when circumstances demand a different approach. Stubborn leaders won't listen, they won't accept feedback, and they don't learn from failures.

Another way of thinking about it is that a leader who is persistent is attached to *the goal*. But a leader who is obstinate is attached to *the ideas* or *ways to reach* that goal.

> A leader who is persistent is attached to the goal. But a leader who is obstinate is attached to the ideas or ways to reach that goal.

The critical difference between persistence and stubbornness lies in your capacity for strategic flexibility. Persistent leaders understand that challenges are part of the leadership journey, and instead of letting them derail their objectives, they approach these setbacks with a problem-solving mindset. Stubborn leaders, however, can become so attached to their original ideas—and most importantly, to the way they believe that their ideas should be accomplished—that they miss opportunities for growth. Worse, they may also risk damaging their teams and organisations overall, simply because they aren't able to adapt.

During the early stages of developing Tesla, Elon Musk faced countless challenges, including financial struggles, technological setbacks, and scepticism from both investors and the public. However, his persistence kept him pushing the boundaries of electric vehicle technology, awareness, and marketing, even when many believed the company was primed to fail. Though the Tesla company is still a work in progress, there's no doubt it's changed the face of EV automobiles and the global automobile industry in general.[24]

Musk would not have been able to achieve this if he'd been stubborn rather than persistent. Stubbornness would have meant ignoring the signals of market changes, technological innovations, or the evolving competitive landscape leading to likely failure. But Musk's persistence was rooted in resilience—adapting, learning from mistakes, and refining his vision over time. And that led to success.

As leaders, we also need to be constantly assessing how we're

---

24 Taylor, E, Shirouzu, N & White, J. (22 July 2020). 'How Tesla defined a new era for the global auto industry.' *Reuters*. https://www.reuters.com/article/technology/how-tesla-defined-a-new-era-for-the-global-auto-industry-idUSKCN24N0GB/#:~:text=Tesla%20would%20go%20on%20to,radical%20thinking%20and%20fast%20innovation.

facing challenges. Are we being persistent, embracing resilience rather than stubbornness? Or are we simply dragging our heels, insisting that our way is *the* way, despite the information we're receiving? Persistence fueled by resilience embraces learning from failure, adjusting plans as needed, and, above all, keeping a clear eye on the long-term goal.

Overcoming Setbacks

In *Game Changer: How John Borghetti Changed the Face of Aviation in Australia*, author Doug Nancarrow chronicles the remarkable career of John Borghetti, who began his journey in the aviation industry as a mailroom clerk at Qantas.[25] Over the next 36 years, Borghetti rose through the ranks at Qantas to eventually become the Executive General Manager. This put him in position to be the next CEO. However, in 2008, the board selected Alan Joyce for the top position instead, which ultimately led to Borghetti leaving the airline.

Despite what could have been a hit to his confidence, Borghetti was undeterred. Demonstrating incredible resilience and unwavering determination, Borghetti embraced a new challenge in 2010 by accepting the CEO position at Virgin Australia. His leadership at Virgin marked a transformative era for the airline and showcased what true resilient leaders can do as Borghetti spearheaded

---

[25] Nancarrow, D. (2015). *Game Changer: How John Borghetti changed the face of aviation in Australia*. HarperSports AU.

Chapter 4: Persist: The Discipline to Stay the Course

Virgin's evolution from a low-cost carrier to a premium airline and a formidable competitor to market-leading Qantas. Under his guidance, Virgin Australia expanded its network, enhanced customer service, and established strategic alliances, ultimately reshaping the competitive landscape of Australian aviation.

Borghetti's journey from an entry-level position to leading a major airline exemplifies persistence in leadership. But it was his ability to overcome setbacks that allowed him to become the leader he needed to be in order to drive significant organisational change. His story also serves as an inspiring testament to the impact of steadfast commitment and visionary leadership in the face of adversity.

> What separates successful leaders from others is their ability to overcome these setbacks without losing sight of their vision and purpose.

Every leader will face setbacks. These could be an unexpected crisis, a financial downturn, or even a personal failure. But what separates successful leaders from others is their ability to overcome these setbacks without losing sight of their vision and purpose.

So how do they do that? There are some key strategies that leaders can use to stay the course even when obstacles arise:

1. **Maintain a clear vision.** Setbacks often test a leader's resolve, and it's easy to lose momentum during tough times. But a leader who has a clear, well-defined vision is able to hold fast and keep their focus on the end goal. They're also better able to keep their team focused on the bigger picture. To maintain a clear vision, you'll need to continually remind yourself and your team why the mission matters and what success looks like in the long term.

2. **Seek feedback and learn from failure.** Setbacks can offer you valuable lessons as a leader. Leaders who persist don't shy away from failure—they learn from it. If you want to be a persistent leader, you'll need to embrace failure as an opportunity to refine your strategies and improve your decision-making. Seek feedback from trusted peers, mentors, or team members who can provide new insights, then use those insights to adapt your decisions and strategies more effectively.

3. **Create a support system.** The weight of leadership can sometimes feel overwhelming, especially when you're facing a setback. A strong support system—whether it's

a team of dedicated individuals, a network of advisors, or family and friends—can provide the emotional and practical support you need to stay the course. As a leader, you can't go it alone. You must be willing to lean on others, delegate tasks, and seek counsel when necessary.

4. **Practice mental toughness.** Mental toughness, or mental resilience, is essential for overcoming setbacks. Mental toughness isn't grinning and bearing it. Instead, it's about maintaining motivation, coping with pressure, concentration, and self-confidence when faced with adversity.[26] Leaders who demonstrate mental toughness can push through doubts and frustrations without losing confidence and can separate the facts from the influences that might distort what they see. You can build mental toughness through meditation, mindfulness practices, or by simply taking time for self-care.[27]

5. **Focus on small wins.** Sometimes the road to success feels overwhelming, especially when things aren't going according to plan. Focusing on small wins along the way, whether that's overcoming a minor challenge or achieving a career-changing milestone—can provide

---

26 Weinberg, R. (3 January 2013). 'Mental toughness: What is it and how to build it.' *Revista da Educação Física*. https://www.researchgate.net/publication/262665458_Mental_toughness_What_is_it_and_how_to_build_it/citation/download.

27 Weinberg. Mental toughness.

the momentum you need to continue to persist, pushing forward towards your vision. Remember to also celebrate those small victories. Soon they'll accumulate to drive larger success.

6. **Embrace adaptability.** While persistence is crucial, it must be coupled with adaptability. As a leader, you must recognise that the world is constantly changing, and strategies that worked in the past may no longer be effective or even viable. You must have the ability and open-mindedness to pivot, adjust your approach, or reframe your thinking when you face a path or a situation that simply isn't working. In this way you'll be able to overcome obstacles and ensure long-term success.

The Mental and Emotional Aspects of Persistence

In *537 Days of Winter*, David Knoff recounts his extraordinary experience as the Station Leader at Antarctica's Davis Research Station.[28] During his time as Station Leader, the team had to manage the onset of the COVID-19 pandemic on top of dealing with the extremes of living in an isolated and harsh environment. Initially scheduled for a standard mission, Knoff and his team of 24 expeditioners faced an unexpected extension of their six-

---

28 Knoff, D. (2022). *537 Days of Winter: Resilience, endurance and humanity while stranded in Antarctica during the pandemic.* Affirm Press.

Chapter 4: Persist: The Discipline to Stay the Course

month stay, which resulted in 537 days of isolation in one of the most extreme environments on Earth.

Leading a team in such unprecedented circumstances required immense emotional and mental resilience. Knoff's leadership philosophy, encapsulated in the phrase 'lead the team you've got, not the team you want,' became crucial as he navigated the challenges of prolonged isolation, uncertainty, and the psychological toll on his team. He had to adapt his leadership style to address the unique needs and dynamics of his team members during an unprecedented time and create a supportive environment that prioritised the team's mental well-being.

> ## Lead the team you've got, not the team you want.

Knoff's leadership helped him maintain morale, manage stress, and keep open communication during an incredibly high-stress situation, and because of this he was able to sustain the team's cohesion and performance throughout those 537 days. When Knoff accepted the position at the Davis Research Station, he prepared and planned, but he simply couldn't have prepared or planned for a pandemic. His story serves as a testament to the importance of leadership resilience in the face of unforeseen challenges.

As Knoff's story shows, leadership persistence is not just a physical or strategic trait—it also involves mental and emotional resilience. Leaders who want to persist through tough times must also navigate the psychological and emotional toll that those challenges can take on themselves. Stress, doubt, frustration, and even burnout are serious risks, and when they rear their heads, can all undermine a leader's ability to stay the course. Understanding and managing the mental and emotional aspects of persistence is the only way to sustain your leadership success when dealing with changes the world can throw at you.

> **Leadership persistence is not just a physical or strategic trait—it also involves mental and emotional resilience.**

How can you better manage the psychological and emotional dramas that can arise from facing challenges?

1. **Managing stress and anxiety.** High levels of stress are often seen as just part of being a leader. And, to

at least some degree, stress is likely to be part of any leadership role, but this is especially true when you face setbacks and challenges. As a leader, you need to learn how to manage your stress effectively or you'll find yourself struggling to make decisions, you'll find it hard to maintain conviction and persistence, and you might even find yourself in burnout. Mindfulness, exercise, and time management techniques can help you as a leader to centre yourself and find calm amidst chaos.

2. **Embracing patience.** Persistence often requires long-term commitment, and success rarely happens overnight. Setbacks are often part of the process as well. So leaders must have the patience to hang on to see results. Patience is the key to allowing you to remain focused on your long-term vision while continuing to make progress in the present.

3. **Dealing with doubt and self-criticism.** Self-doubt and negative self-talk can be huge obstacles when a leader is striving to stay persistent. Research by the National Science Foundation found that the average person has between 12,000 and 60,000 thoughts per day, and of those, about 80% are negative.[29] This kind of thinking as a leader can undermine confidence and erode resolve. To counteract this, leaders must develop a healthy level

---

29 Simone, F. (4 December 2017). 'Negative Self-Talk: Don't Let It Overwhelm You.' *Psychology Today.* https://www.psychologytoday.com/au/blog/family-affair/201712/negative-self-talk-dont-let-it-overwhelm-you.

of self-compassion. Practicing positive self-affirmation is a good way to build this self-compassion, and it allows you to recognise that setbacks are not a reflection of personal failure but a natural part of the leadership journey. This is key to mental persistence.

4. **Staying connected to purpose.** Persistence can be emotionally taxing, especially when you're facing long-term challenges. Getting to your vision starts to feel like a hard slog rather than a clear path. But leaders who maintain a deep connection to their sense of purpose, mission, or the larger cause they are working towards are better able to persevere through difficult times. Keeping that 'why' at the front of mind will help provide motivation to push through to the end even when things seem bleak.

Persisting Through Adversity

I have always taken pride in my ability to excel based on merit rather than by pandering to superiors for opportunities. This approach is fulfilling, but it's not always the easiest way to succeed, and I often found myself as the second choice for roles I really wanted and felt I deserved. One of these experiences stands out, when there was the opportunity to raise a new helicopter squadron from scratch.

It wasn't just important to create a new squadron. The leader who

Chapter 4: Persist: The Discipline to Stay the Course

took on the role needed to be able to create a squadron that could perform mission-critical operations. The squadron's mission was critical because it would be tasked with training and delivering pilots who were waiting for conversions to other aircraft types. It was also going to be established adjacent to a special operations helicopter unit, a role I believed I was well-suited for.

Initially, I missed out on the role. The position went to someone I knew was already preparing to leave the military for a civilian career. Despite this setback, I stayed positive and committed to my work. But when the officer who was originally given the role resigned shortly afterwards, the opportunity went to me. I was thrilled, and I poured everything I had into the job, excelling to the point where I was recognised as the highest-performing major in the Aviation Corps. My efforts were further validated when I was awarded the prestigious Army Aviator of the Year. But I would never have achieved these accomplishments if I hadn't been able to persist through adversity.

Of course, that wasn't the only challenge that I faced. Even with those accomplishments under my belt, I found myself as a reserve for attendance at the Australian Command and Staff College, a premier military education institution that provides advanced professional military education and leadership training for officers of the Australian Defence Force to prepare them for senior leadership roles. Out of 170 spots, only four were allocated to Army pilots. I was ranked fifth. Once again, I remained patient and committed to my work, and when one of the selected pilots resigned to take a civilian helicopter job, I stepped in.

That year at staff college was one of the most intense periods of my career. It wasn't just about military training. We were also required to complete a master's degree in military strategy and leadership from the Australian National University. Having never attended university before, I found myself struggling with a steep learning curve. The combination of academic demands and military training left me with very little room for doing anything else, including rest. But I stayed disciplined and focused, and by the end of the year, I graduated in the top 15 Army students, outperforming the other three pilots who had initially been selected over me.

After staff college, I was assigned as a military adviser to a general. This role was a significant milestone in my military career, and it paved the way for my eventual promotion to Lieutenant Colonel. But even after achieving this rank, I wasn't the first choice for unit command. And when I was passed over again, it felt like another setback. But I knew that if I stayed focused and determined, my consistent performance and commitment would eventually be recognised.

In time, I was selected as the Commanding Officer of the Australian Defence Force Helicopter School. This was a position that carried immense responsibility. However, in order to take on this role, I needed to become a qualified flying instructor. Becoming

Chapter 4: Persist: The Discipline to Stay the Course

an instructor is a specialised career stream that officers usually enter at a more junior rank, such as Captain. Those who pursue this path typically remain within the instructional stream for most of their careers. Because my career had followed a different trajectory, focused on operational command and leadership, I had not previously undertaken this qualification.

Stepping into the Commanding Officer role of the Australian Defence Force (ADF) Helicopter School required me to pivot and complete the certification at the more senior rank of Lieutenant Colonel, a path that's uncommon and significantly more demanding due to the dual responsibility of leading a large, high-performing unit while simultaneously meeting the intense technical and instructional standards required of an instructor pilot. I had to prepare to lead a unit of over 300 personnel, 20 helicopters, and a combination of military and civilian staff while simultaneously undertaking rigorous instructor training. This was a demanding workload that required me to balance high-stakes leadership with intensive personal development.

Within my unit, I was responsible for overseeing airworthiness, technical worthiness, and the safety management system for complex flying operations, as well as personnel management, operational planning, and contractual oversight of civilian maintenance teams.

At the same time, I had to maintain a demanding flying schedule that had me in the air day and night so that I could meet the requirements of my instructor qualification and manage my role as Chief Pilot and Chief Instructor of the organisation. The demands were relentless, and to meet them while leading effectively *and* mastering the technical and instructional competencies required for the role, I had to have exceptional time management, resilience, and adaptability.

I managed this and even excelled in this role because of my persistence. I would not give up because I knew that these challenges and this time spent pushing through hard things would actually help me become a better leader with a problem-solving mindset. And I knew I would need that to continue to rise in my military career.

It must have worked. As a result of my performance as the Commanding Officer of the Australian Defence Force Helicopter School, I was posted to the Pentagon as the United States Marine Corps Liaison Officer. This position was traditionally reserved for infantry officers, not aviation, but for the first time in my career, I was the first choice. It was a role that required resilience, adaptability, and a deep understanding of leadership. And I felt lucky that these were all qualities I had refined through years of perseverance as I faced setbacks and challenges.

Reflection on Persistence

Through these experiences, I learned the true value of persistence and developed the discipline to stay the course. Every setback taught me to remain focused on my long-term goals, adapt when necessary, and trust that hard work would eventually pay off. I learned for myself that persistence is not about being stubborn—it's about being resilient in your convictions. It's about being able to bounce back, learn from failure, and stay the course even when the odds seem against you.

For myself, the road was never easy, and it's unlikely to be so for you either in your leadership roles. But by maintaining focus, seeking opportunities to grow, and remaining adaptable, I was able to turn setbacks into stepping stones for success—and so will you.

In leadership, challenges are inevitable. What defines us is how we respond to them. For me, persistence wasn't just about staying in the fight. It was about staying sharp, staying ready, and seizing every opportunity that came my way despite being in the fight. Rather than pushing me off my path, each challenge reinforced my commitment to my purpose, and ultimately I was able to see my goals come to fruition. The path to success often lies just beyond the obstacles we are willing to overcome.

Takeaways

Persistence is more than just the ability to keep going. It's the disciplined, strategic determination to stay the course, despite setbacks, uncertainty, and adversity. Resilient leaders recognise that failure is often the precursor to success and that setbacks provide the necessary lessons for growth. By embracing the mental, emotional, and strategic aspects of persistence, leaders can transform challenges into opportunities and continue moving towards their long-term goals.

Whether you're navigating a crisis, working through a failure, or building a team to face an uncertain future, persistence is your most reliable ally. It's the bridge between where you are now and where you're headed, a trait that, when nurtured, can turn potential into success and vision into reality.

Call to Action

As a leader, your ability to persist is not defined by how long you hold the line but by how intentionally you hold it. Before charging forward or digging in deeper, take a moment to pause, reflect, and realign.

Use the following tool as your checkpoint, your moment of clarity to reconnect with who you are, what you're facing, and why it matters. Ask yourself the hard questions. Because true leadership isn't blind endurance. It's disciplined persistence with purpose.

Chapter 4: Persist: The Discipline to Stay the Course

Tool: Persist with Purpose—A Leader's Table for Strategic Discipline

This tool is designed to help you, as a leader, assess whether you're demonstrating disciplined persistence—or simply digging in out of pride or fear.

Strategic Filter	Key Question	Character (integrity and humility)	Courage (facing discomfort and truth)	Conviction (purpose and values-driven)	Persist If ✓	Rethink If ✗
Clarity	Am I clear on the outcome, and is it still relevant?	You're honest about whether the action still serves the mission.	You're willing to admit if the situation has changed.	You've confirmed the action aligns with your values and the broader vision.	The goal is still valid, timely, and strategically sound.	The goal was set under outdated assumptions or is no longer aligned.
Purpose	Am I doing this for the right reason or to prove something?	You check your ego and focus on impact over your image.	You face the discomfort of acknowledging missteps.	You're serving something greater than yourself.	Your persistence is mission-focused, not self-serving.	You're stuck defending your pride, not your purpose.
Flexibility	Am I open to adapting the *how*, even if I stay firm on the *why*?	You listen deeply and stay open to new approaches.	You act on feedback, even when it challenges your assumptions.	You stay anchored in your *why*, not your methods.	You're adapting while staying true to your vision.	You're clinging to a method that no longer works.

How to Use This Tool

When you hit resistance, setbacks, or internal doubt:

1. Pause and reflect using the three key questions.
2. Anchor your reflection in character (who am I in this?), courage (what must I face?), and conviction (why does this matter?).

Why It Matters

Persistence without clarity becomes noise. Persistence without purpose becomes ego. Persistence without flexibility becomes failure. But persistence guided by character, courage, and conviction? That becomes leadership.

CHAPTER 5

Pivot: The Art of Adaptability

Recognising When Change is Necessary

One of the core skills of a successful leader is the ability to recognise when change is needed and take decisive action to pivot. We've talked about adaptability already as part of the other pillars of our framework. But adaptability plays a bigger part—it's not just part of other pillars, it's a pillar itself. That's because in today's fast-paced, ever-evolving business and societal landscapes, adaptability is no longer optional. It's a critical survival skill for everyone, but especially for leaders and organisations.

The first step in mastering the art of pivoting is learning to recognise when things are no longer working. This could be a strategy that no longer yields results, an initiative that has lost its relevance, or an approach that is stifling growth. This is often trickier than we might think, because it requires us to continuously review what we've been doing and let go of our ego enough to really see when what we've been doing hasn't been working.

In today's fast-paced, ever-evolving business and societal landscapes, adaptability is no longer optional.

While the ability to identify these moments of stagnation and act decisively is a hallmark of high-impact leadership, the challenge lies in distinguishing between momentary obstacles and systemic issues. A momentary obstacle could be a temporary dip in sales or an unforeseen market shift. These kinds of problems are typically easy to overcome with persistence and slight adjustments. A systemic issue, however, indicates a deeper misalignment within your business environment or with your goals, and because of that, it requires a bigger and more strategic pivot.

Whether you're facing a momentary obstacle or a systemic issue, to pivot effectively as a leader, you'll need to be able to respond to real, informed insights (typically the kind you'd receive through

Chapter 5: Pivot: The Art of Adaptability

data, feedback, or obtaining a deeper understanding of industry trends). You can't respond impulsively, but you also can't wait too long to adapt. The first might see you making rash decisions, while the second might result in missed opportunities, increased risks, or total failure.

Netflix is a great example of effective pivoting. When it was founded, DVDs were the cutting-edge technology for at-home movie viewing, and Netflix was one of the first DVD rental services. But the leadership team, particularly co-founders Marc Randolph and Reed Hastings, recognised early on that the future of entertainment was digital.[30] Randolph said, 'I don't think either of us really thought [DVD rentals were] going to last more than five or six years.'[31]

So in 2007, almost a decade after sending its first DVD in the mail, Netflix pivoted and launched its streaming service. At the time, this was a massive shift that required abandoning a highly successful business model in favour of an untested one. However, their early recognition of changing technology allowed them to seize the opportunity, and today they're one of the dominant players in the media industry.

---

30 Meyer, E & Hastings, R. (2020). *No Rules: Netflix and the Culture of Reinvention.* Penguin Press.
31 Fell, J. (30 September 2023). 'Netflix's DVD business almost didn't exist. Twenty-five years on, it has transformed the media industry.' *News.* https://www.abc.net.au/news/2023-09-30/netflix-shutters-dvd-delivery-marc-randolph/102902864.

Pivoting to Save the Mission

Pivoting and adapting has certainly been part of my own career. My first non-executive director appointment to the board of a not-for-profit boutique hotel was a good bridge between my military work and my corporate work.

The hotel was a well-intentioned social enterprise, and I was excited to be part of it. But during my very first board meeting, I uncovered a systemic issue that threatened the future of the organisation.

During that board meeting, I reviewed the financial report, and noted that a qualification had been placed on our accounts. This immediately raised red flags for me, so I dug deeper and was stunned to learn that the qualification stemmed from the non-renewal of the hotel's charitable status when the Goods and Services Tax (GST) was introduced. This oversight had continued for years, and it was significant enough that the board had been setting aside funds in case the tax office required back payments. But despite the growing risks, the board was reluctant to address the issue.

This situation presented an opportunity disguised as a challenge. The hotel was underperforming financially, largely due to deferred maintenance and neglect, and it desperately needed a major renovation. Situated in a prime beachfront location, the property had immense potential to generate sustainable income.

However, its charitable operations were likely no longer feasible under the current business model.

It was while we were working on developing the board's strategic plan that I saw the opportunity to propose a bold pivot. Rather than clinging to the status quo, we could transform the business model in a way that would secure the hotel's long-term future. I suggested that if we were not able to regain charitable status, we could partner with a developer to rebuild the hotel into a modern facility. This new model would allow us to lease rooms to a larger and more diverse customer base, which would then generate the revenue needed to maintain and even renovate the property and fulfil our mission.

Some of the board resisted my suggested strategic pivot. There was concern that moving away from a purely charitable model would compromise the hotel's purpose. Others were wary of the risks involved in pursuing a redevelopment project. To gain buy-in, I emphasised that the proposed changes would enable us to expand our impact rather than abandon it. By improving the hotel's facilities and financial performance, we could continue providing affordable accommodation to our core audience while serving a broader clientele and making the entire project financially viable.

The pivot also aligned perfectly with the review of our strategic plan, facilities plan, marketing plan, and risk management framework, which we were undertaking at the same time. This presented a rare opportunity to address the financial qualification, implement long-overdue renovations, and create a sustainable business model all at once.

It took persistent leadership, transparent and continuous communication, and detailed planning, but eventually I was able to guide the board towards considering this new direction. Of course, the change wouldn't be immediate. It required careful negotiation, partnerships with external stakeholders, and the development of a clear execution plan. However, the pivot would ultimately set the hotel on a path to financial stability and operational excellence, allowing us to continue providing affordable accommodation to service members while adapting to the realities of a changing world.

> By being adaptable, you can turn even the most daunting challenges into platforms for innovation and progress.

This experience taught me that adaptability is not just about reacting to challenges. That's important, of course, but as leaders, we also need to be able to proactively identify opportunities for growth *in spite of* adversity. Adaptability allows you to embrace change, seeing it as an opportunity to make decisions that bring your operations more in line with your organisation's core vision. By being adaptable, you can, as a leader, turn even the most daunting challenges into platforms for innovation and progress.

How to Shift Strategy Without Losing Momentum

Once the need for change has been identified, the next step is to execute a pivot without losing momentum. Pivoting doesn't mean abandoning all your previous efforts but rather adjusting your course in response to change while maintaining the core purpose and values of your organisation.

While it sounds simple, it can be challenging to adapt well and keep your eye on the long-term vision. So, here are some key strategies for executing a pivot with continued forward movement:

1. **Reassess your core vision.** Before making any strategic changes, it's essential to take a step back and reassess the core vision of your organisation. Do you still have this at the forefront of all your decisions? And is it still aligned with the organisation's goals? Sometimes, a pivot is also an opportunity to refine your original vision, strengthening it for the future.

2. **Clear communication.** Pivoting in response to change often requires buy-in from key stakeholders, including your team, customers, investors, and partners. And to ensure this buy-in, clear, transparent communication between yourself and those stakeholders is vital. You'll need to be able to explain the reasons behind the pivot, the benefits it will bring, and the steps involved in making it successful. When you can provide this context, you can create alignment with the vision and reduce the worry that comes from uncertainty.

3. **Leverage existing resources.** A successful pivot doesn't require starting from scratch. Instead, leaders should leverage their existing resources, strengths, and competencies to shift direction without losing forward momentum. When you can capitalise on existing assets—whether that's brand recognition, customer loyalty, or established systems—you'll be able to maintain momentum and make the transition more seamless.

4. **Start small, test, and learn.** A pivot doesn't have to be a massive overhaul. It can (and typically should) begin with a small-scale trial or by taking just a first step. Start by testing the new strategy with a limited audience or in a specific region. Then gather feedback, measure the results, and refine the strategy as needed. An iterative approach will allow you to pivot effectively while minimising risk or error or miscalculation.

5. **Maintain focus on execution.** As your strategy changes and develops, it's important not to lose focus on execution. You may be exploring new opportunities or shifting directions, but you need to ensure that your day-to-day operations continue to run smoothly, as this will support your ability to meet your new goals. To keep the pressure on both fronts, however, you'll need to delegate tasks effectively, monitor progress, and maintain a high level of accountability. This is the only way to ensure that both the pivot and the day-to-day business that keeps the lights on are executed efficiently.

6. **Stay agile and open to further adjustments.** A pivot is not a one-time event—it's an ongoing process of adjustment and improvement. Stay agile and open to making further shifts as you collect data, gather insights, and experience new challenges. This mindset of continual improvement enables you to stay ahead of the curve and avoid becoming stagnant or left behind.

Types of Pivots

While a pivot typically refers to a change in strategy, there are different types of pivots. These can range from tactical to strategic. Understanding the distinction between these two is essential for leaders to navigate change effectively.

Tactical pivots

A tactical pivot involves adjusting specific actions or processes while staying aligned with the overall strategy. It could be tweaking a marketing approach, altering the way a product is delivered, or shifting focus to a different target audience. Tactical pivots are often driven by short-term needs and external factors but don't drastically alter the larger direction of the organisation.

For example, during the COVID-19 pandemic, many companies made tactical pivots in response to the sudden disruption of business operations. Restaurants switched to online delivery, retailers shifted to e-commerce, and manufacturers repurposed their facilities to produce PPE. These tactical pivots allowed companies to survive during a crisis but did not fundamentally change the business model.

Strategic transformations

A strategic transformation, on the other hand, involves a more profound shift in direction and requires a long-term commitment to new goals. It may involve entering a new market, creating an entirely new product line, or redefining the company's value proposition. Strategic transformations are often driven by long-term trends, technological innovations, or shifts in customer expectations.

Strategic transformations require more planning, resources, and often a cultural shift within the organisation. Leaders must be prepared to lead the charge with conviction, ensuring that the entire organisation is aligned with the new direction.

Lessons from Apple: Tactical Pivots vs Strategic Transformations

Apple remains in the upper echelon of companies that have and continue to pivot in what is a rapidly changing industry (perhaps the most rapidly changing). In *Tim Cook: The Genius Who Took Apple to the Next Level,* author Leander Kahney delves into the leadership strategies that propelled Apple to unprecedented heights.[32]

Many were surprised when Tim Cook, the intensely private executive who many viewed as Apple's 'operations drone', was tapped to fill the CEO role after Jobs. But it was under his leadership, and his adaptive leadership at that, that Apple became the world's first trillion-dollar company.

Two notable examples of Cook's adaptive leadership were his tactical pivot towards environmental sustainability and his strategic pivot in expanding Apple's services division.

---

32 Kahney, L. (2019). *Tim Cook: The Genius Who Took Apple to the Next Level.* Portfolio.

Tactical Pivot—Environmental Sustainability Initiatives

Recognising the growing importance of corporate responsibility to consumers, Cook initiated a tactical shift by embedding environmental sustainability into Apple's operations. In particular, he implemented a closed-loop supply chain to better reduce electronic waste. This pivot not only enhanced Apple's brand reputation but also resonated with environmentally conscious consumers, a large part of Apple's young consumer demographic. Cook's pivot brought Apple's operational practices in line with changing societal values.

Strategic Pivot—Expansion into Services

Cook saw that the market would soon be saturated with hardware options, competitors, and sales. In response, he orchestrated a strategic pivot by expanding Apple's focus to include a robust services division. This shift led to the development and growth of services like Apple Music, Apple Pay, and the App Store, which diversified Apple's revenue streams and reduced the company's dependence on hardware sales. This strategic pivot put Apple in the position to capitalise on the burgeoning digital services market and ensured its sustained growth and profitability.

Lessons from Apple

These pivots exemplify Cook's adaptive leadership, and showcase his ability to navigate the company through evolving industry landscapes by implementing both immediate tactical changes and long-term strategic shifts. These are also lessons we should take into our own leadership. Like Cook, we need to be agile enough to change our focus and strategy when needed, and committed enough to our purpose to bring our team along as well.

Takeaways

The ability to pivot in the face of change is an essential skill for modern leaders. It requires the ability to recognise when change is necessary, execute a strategy shift without losing momentum, and maintain focus on long-term success. It doesn't really matter whether the pivot is a tactical adjustment or you're undergoing a full strategic transformation—the key to a successful pivot always lies in adaptability, strategic thinking, and strong leadership.

In the fast-changing business world, the ability to pivot effectively is what separates high-impact leaders from those who stagnate or fail. Leaders who can pivot successfully are able to navigate challenges with confidence, maintain alignment with their core vision, and keep their teams moving forward towards their goals. The art of pivoting is not about abandoning one's vision but refining it in the face of new information and changing circumstances.

 Call to Action

Leadership isn't about stubbornly holding the course—it's about knowing when to adjust it. When change comes knocking, don't react. Pause. Reflect. Pivot with purpose.

Use this tool to examine the challenge in front of you, ground yourself in truth, and choose a path that aligns with who you are and where you're going. Check your character to release ego, summon your courage to face discomfort, and lean into your conviction to ensure the pivot still serves your mission.

Chapter 5: Pivot: The Art of Adaptability

Tool: Pivot with Purpose—A Leader's Guide to Adaptability in Action

Successful pivots aren't reactive—they're *intentional*. This tool helps leaders determine when, why, and how to adapt by examining the type of challenge, the reason for change, and the best-fit response.

Strategic Filter	Key Question	Character (integrity and humility)	Courage (facing discomfort and truth)	Conviction (purpose and values-driven)	Persist If ✓	Rethink If ✗
Recognition	Is this a momentary obstacle or a deeper issue?	You're honest about what's not working, even if it's your idea.	You seek feedback and confront hard truths.	The issue is pulling you away from your core mission.	Path is unsustainable or no longer aligned.	You haven't done the work to diagnose the root cause.
Motivation	Am I pivoting for growth or avoiding discomfort?	You examine your intent with self-awareness.	You act despite fear of criticism or failure.	The change advances the mission, not ego or trend.	You're choosing progress over pride.	You're chasing a shortcut or reacting emotionally.
Scope	Is this a tactical shift or a strategic transformation?	You accept the ripple effect of change.	You engage your team and stakeholders openly.	The new direction strengthens your long-term impact.	You've matched the scale of change to the size of the problem.	You're overcorrecting or misjudging the risk.

How to Use This Tool

Before making a change:

1. **Check your character.** Are you being honest with yourself and your team?
2. **Act with courage.** Are you facing what needs to be faced?
3. **Hold your conviction.** Is the pivot still true to your mission?

Why It Matters

Character helps you let go of ego. Courage helps you step into the unknown. Conviction helps you stay the course—even when the course changes.

Pivoting isn't a weakness. It's wisdom in motion. Using this tool will help you embrace this skill in your own leadership.

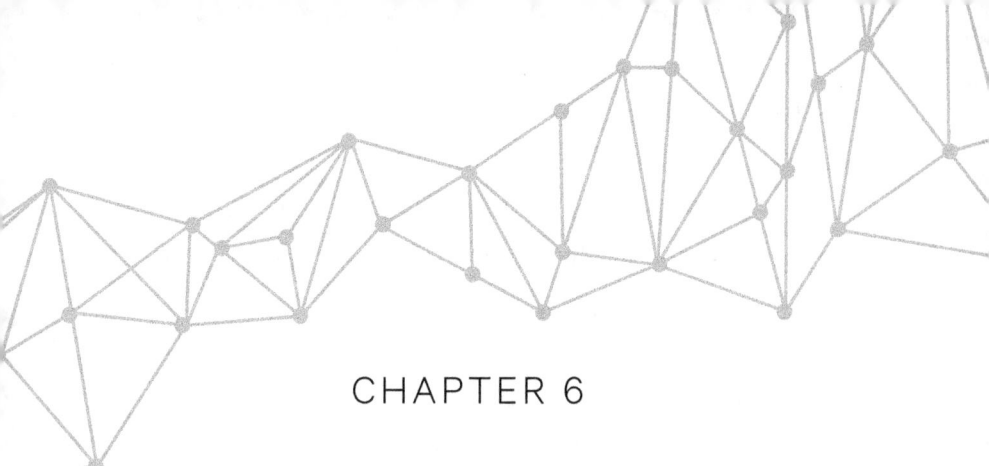

CHAPTER 6

Part-With: The Power of Letting Go

Recognising When It's Time to Move On

For high-impact leaders, one of the most challenging but important skills is knowing when it's time to let go. Whether it's a strategy, initiative, or team member, understanding when something no longer serves the organisation's greater good (or worse, is undermining it) is key to becoming a leader that can take an organisation into the future.

Unfortunately, letting go can be tough, especially when there's an emotional attachment to a particular strategy or team member. As humans we don't like letting go because of a combination of psychological, emotional and especially learned behaviour.[33] But often it comes down to fear—fear of change, fear of failure, and, particularly, fear of the unknown.

One of the most challenging but important skills is knowing when it's time to let go.

Acknowledging that something or someone is no longer aligned with your organisation's long-term goals requires strength, but it's also the mark of an effective leader. It's the ability to make difficult decisions that sets true leadership apart from those who are really just acting as managers.

Knowing when to part with something requires a clear understanding of the bigger picture. As a leader, you need to be looking out for these situations by undertaking regular assessments of strategies, initiatives, and people and reflecting on whether they remain aligned with your organisation's evolving goals and long-term vision. Regular reviews should keep you up to date, but when progress stalls and resources aren't yielding

---

33 le Cunff, A. (28 December 2023). 'Ness Labs: The Art and Science of Letting Go.' Ness Labs. https://newsletter.nesslabs.com/posts/ness-labs-the-art-and-science-of-letting-go#:~:text=We%20also%20tend%20to%20cling,similar%20situations%20in%20the%20future.

returns, or when an individual's performance is consistently lacking, you'll also need to conduct a pointed review at that time. Continuing down the same path can do more harm than good.

The Psychology of Detachment in Leadership

Letting go isn't always about failure—it's about growth. It's making space for new ideas, strategies, and individuals who are better suited to move the organisation forward. But letting go is as much a psychological process as it is a strategic one. And leaders recognise that to truly progress, they must let go of any emotional response so they can release what no longer contributes to their vision.

> ### Letting go isn't always about failure—it's about growth.

However, leaders often struggle emotionally when the decision involves individuals or initiatives once vital to the organisation—or that they had a big part in conceptualising or implementing. As humans (and as leaders) we have a deep attachment to past choices, making the process of detachment particularly hard.

However, understanding the psychological dynamics that might hold us back from detaching from past choices can help leaders let go of those emotions and be able to make decisions with clarity and confidence. It's normal to worry about making changes. The fear of making the wrong decision or the guilt of letting someone go can weigh heavily on you as a leader, particularly in the short term. So the key to moving through that is to shift your perspective to the long-term vision and the beneficial impact the change will make. Rather than focusing on the negatives that might come from change (and any change has friction), focus on how letting go will allow you to refocus the team's energy and resources on areas that will drive future success.

It's also essential to recognise that letting go is not a personal failure—it's an acknowledgement that the current approach, strategy, or personnel no longer works. Detaching emotionally allows decisions to be based on facts and the organisation's needs, rather than on personal biases or sentimental attachments.

> **Letting go is not a personal failure—it's an acknowledgement that the current approach, strategy, or personnel no longer works.**

The process is often just as challenging for those affected, whether it's a long-term employee, an underperforming team member, or letting go of an outdated business strategy that has become part of the fixture of your team. As a leader, you'll need to approach these transitions with empathy, showing respect for past contributions and solutions while making it clear that the new approach is part of the organisation's evolution and will be the way forward.

Letting Go to Save a Life and Inspire Change

The power of letting go has never been more apparent than during my time in the United States. When I was with the Pentagon, I was entrusted with a critical foreign position, representing Australia in a role that demanded the utmost professionalism and resilience. I was proud of what I had achieved at that stage. My career was on an upward trajectory, and there was a promotion waiting back in Australia. It was everything I had worked for over the past 25 years, and I was proud to be in a career that defined my identity and purpose.

But like many in the armed forces, things under the surface weren't as rosy as they seemed. One evening, while flying from Washington, D.C. to Los Angeles, the weight of my experiences in the military came crashing down on me. I broke down in tears on the flight, overwhelmed by emotions that I couldn't hold back any longer. I was embarrassed. I hid my tears and waited until I arrived in L.A. to call my wife. Her words on the other end of the line were simple but direct—'You need professional help.'

She was right. Not long after, I was diagnosed with post-traumatic stress disorder (PTSD) stemming from my operational service. While this might seem obvious to people looking from the outside, I refused to accept this diagnosis. For 25 years, I had served my country, demonstrating strength, resilience, and leadership. For me to admit vulnerability felt like a betrayal of everything I stood for. It felt like failure. I was in denial, unwilling to take medication or commit to any treatment. Instead, I convinced myself that I could fight through this alone, just as I had always done in the past.

But I couldn't. And day by day things got harder and harder, until eventually the struggle became unbearable, and I found myself in a hospital bed after attempting to take my own life. My superiors, peers, and subordinates had witnessed my visible deterioration, and many were aware of my struggle to hold on. But no one had understood how bad it really was, because I hadn't been vulnerable enough to share that with them. The day I woke up in the hospital, we all realised how bad it really was. And it was a turning point—not only for me but for those around me as well.

Eventually, I realised I needed to let go of the career that had defined me. Clinging to the military while ignoring the toll it had taken and was continuing to take on my mental health was just not sustainable. In fact, it was life-threatening. I made the incredibly difficult decision to part with my military career and focus on my rehabilitation and my family. It felt like a failure at the time—like my psychology was defeating me. But with the power of hindsight, I now know it was the decision that saved my life.

Over time I came to realise something else. Letting go was not just an act of self-preservation—it was an act of leadership. Laying bare my struggle paved the way for others to reflect on and even open up about their own challenges. And making the decision to let go of my military career laid the foundation for others to let go of things that might not be the right thing in their own lives. By openly confronting my vulnerability, I showed my peers and subordinates that seeking help and letting go of something no longer serving you is not a sign of weakness—it's a step towards growth and healing.

As leaders, we often feel compelled to persevere at all costs. But true leadership lies in the ability to make tough decisions for the greater good of yourself, your team, and the organisation. So letting go is not about failure. It's about creating the space necessary for growth, innovation, and a brighter future.

My decision to part with my military career ultimately allowed me to rediscover my purpose and focus on what truly mattered—my health and my family. But importantly, it also opened up space for me to find my next chapter, proving that sometimes, the greatest strength lies in the courage to release the past.

Restructuring, Resignations, and Realignment for Long-Term Success

Letting go also plays a crucial role in restructuring and realigning an organisation for future success. As the business environment shifts, so must the organisation's structure, teams, and objectives.

In some cases, a complete strategic realignment may be necessary to truly let go and create space for something new. In his autobiography, *Losing My Virginity*, Richard Branson recounts a significant strategic realignment at Virgin Group during the early 1990s.[34] Facing intense competition from British Airways and financial pressures within the Virgin Group, Branson made the decision to sell Virgin Records, the company's flagship music label, to EMI for $1 billion. This bold move allowed him to focus resources on Virgin Atlantic, his burgeoning airline venture, which he believed had greater long-term potential. It was a decision that paid off by helping him build his $2.5 billion net worth and, as he said, 'I don't think I would have gone to space on my own spaceship if I hadn't made that decision.'[35]

Branson's willingness to part with a successful yet resource-consuming entity to strategically invest in a sector poised for

---

34 Branson, R. (2011). *Losing My Virginity: How I Survived, Had Fun, and Made a Fortune Doing Business My Way.* Crown Currency.
35 Huddleston, T. (29 April 2024). 'Richard Branson says this decision helped build his $2.5B net worth: "I don't think I would have gone to space' otherwise."' *CNBC.* https://www.cnbc.com/2024/04/29/richard-branson-tough-business-decision-helped-me-build-virgin-group.html.

future growth made a huge difference to the ultimate success of Virgin Group. Just like Branson, effective leaders understand that parting ways can open the door to new opportunities and innovations. And although these changes can be uncomfortable, they can strengthen the organisation and better position it for the future.

Takeaways

Leaders who embrace the power of letting go create space for fresh ideas, new talent, and strategies better suited to the organisation's evolving needs and often more supportive to their own needs as well. By making decisions based on data and facts, leaders can navigate these transitions with clarity and confidence.

Leaders who are willing to part with what no longer serves them show a commitment to adaptability and growth. They understand that letting go is not about failure—it's about making room for a brighter, more prosperous future.

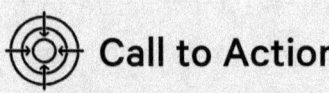
Call to Action

Leadership is not just about what you hold onto— it's also about what you have the wisdom to release. Before you let go of a plan, position, relationship, or even an outdated version of yourself, pause and reflect with purpose.

Use this tool to check your character. Are you being honest about its true value? Are you acting with courage by being willing to release what no longer serves you or your mission? Are you leaning into your conviction by creating space for growth, clarity, and forward movement?

Letting go is not a loss. It's a deliberate act of leadership. It's not a weakness. It's making room for what's next.

Tool: Part with Purpose—A Leader's Guide to Letting Go with Character, Courage, and Conviction

Letting go isn't weakness—it's wisdom. This tool helps leaders decide *what* to release, *when* to release it, and *why*.

Chapter 6: Part-With: The Power of Letting Go

Leadership isn't about stubbornly holding the course—it's about knowing when to adjust it.

Strategic Filter	Key Question	Character (integrity and humility)	Courage (facing discomfort and truth)	Conviction (purpose and values-driven)	Persist If ✓	Rethink If ✗
Alignment	Is this still serving our purpose, people, or potential?	You're willing to acknowledge what's no longer working.	You face the discomfort of detaching from something familiar.	Letting go creates space to better serve your core mission.	It no longer aligns with your vision, goals, or values.	It still holds strategic relevance and potential with adjustment.
Impact	Is holding on helping or harming?	You evaluate results with integrity, not sentiment.	You accept that clinging on may be causing more harm than good.	Releasing it enables growth and renewal elsewhere.	Performance, trust, or energy is being consistently drained.	Challenges are short-term and improvement is still possible.
Readiness	Am I emotionally and operationally prepared to move on?	You detach ego from the outcome and lead with empathy.	You're ready to act despite personal or political risk.	You're clear this decision supports a better future.	You've built a clear transition plan and communicated it openly.	You're acting from impulse or fear rather than reflection.

PART 2: The Adaptive Leadership Model—P3

How to Use This Tool

Before letting go of a person, plan, position, or past version of your strategies, operations, or even yourself:

1. **Check your character.** Are you being honest about the real value it's adding?
2. **Act with courage.** Are you facing what needs to be released?
3. **Lean into conviction.** Does letting go move you closer to your purpose?

Why It Matters

Character gives you the humility to acknowledge when it's time.

Courage gives you the strength to let go — even when it hurts.

Conviction keeps you focused on the future, not attached to the past.

Letting go is not giving up. It's giving space for what's next.

PART 3

Applying C3P3 to Leadership, Strategy, and Performance

In this final part of our book, we bring the C3P3 Leadership Framework to life by focusing on its practical application. You can think of this as the nuts and bolts of integrating the six foundational pillars into your real-world leadership.

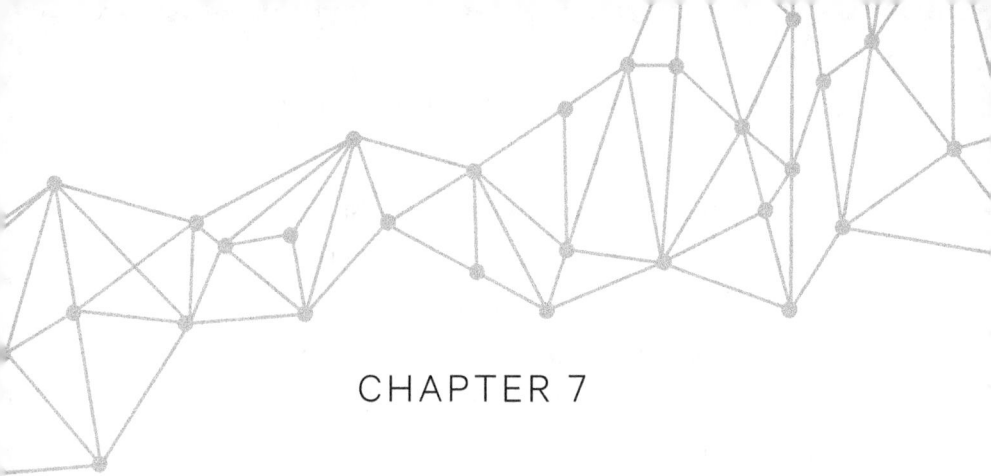

CHAPTER 7

C3P3 in Action

Leading with the C3P3 Framework

As a leader, you will face opportunities and challenges. The value in this is that they can show you what you're made of and the areas where you might need to improve. That's because the true test of leadership emerges not in routine management but in how you respond to those opportunities and challenges so that you can always remain one step ahead.

The C3P3 framework—character, courage, conviction, persistence, pivot, and part-with—provides a structured, holistic approach that can empower you with tools to navigate leadership with clarity, agility, and a steadfast commitment to your organisation's long-term success.

PART 3: Applying C3P3 to Leadership, Strategy, and Performance

When you embrace and integrate these six core principles into your leadership, you'll create a robust foundation that can guide your decision-making while maintaining stakeholder trust. Most importantly, you'll be in a position to see your organisation through any opportunity or challenge it might face, help safeguard its future, and drive its growth.

Each pillar within the framework plays a distinct yet complementary leadership role:

- **Character** establishes the moral foundation, ensuring decisions are anchored in enduring ethical values.
- **Courage** drives bold action, inspiring leaders to confront uncertainty and make difficult choices.
- **Conviction** reinforces a resolute adherence to a long-term vision, even amidst chaos.
- **Persistence** fuels the relentless pursuit of solutions despite setbacks.
- **Pivot** embodies the flexibility to adapt strategies when circumstances shift.
- **Part-with** represents the willingness to shed outdated practices or relationships that hinder progress.

Real-World Applications of C3P3

Character in Action—The Tylenol Crisis

In 1982, Johnson and Johnson confronted a severe public health crisis when cyanide-laced Tylenol capsules led to several fatalities. Demonstrating unwavering character, the company prioritised consumer safety over short-term profits by recalling 31 million bottles of Tylenol.

This was a decisive, ethically driven response that not only restored public trust but also set a benchmark in leadership for other companies to follow.

Courage in Action—The Chilean Miners Rescue

There's unlikely to be anyone in Australia who wasn't aware of and closely following the fate of the 33 miners trapped 2,000 feet underground during the 2010 mine collapse in Chile. And there would have been no one world-wide who wasn't impressed by President Sebastián Piñera's courageous leadership as he organised and catalysed the truly historic rescue effort.[36]

Despite daunting uncertainties and immense pressure, his bold decisions and transparent communication galvanised both national and international support. This had an incredible result,

---

36 Franklin, J. (2011). *The 33: The Ultimate Account of the Chilean Miners Dramatic Rescue.* Transworld Digital.

with all 33 miners ultimately being successfully rescued after an incredible 69 days underground. It also demonstrated the vital role of courage in leadership.

Conviction in Action—Winston Churchill During WWII

The British Empire existed for nearly half a millennium. It spread across the face of the world, from America to Australia,[37] but in 1940, with the Nazis marching across Europe, Britain was facing imminent defeat. It was in this moment of crisis that Winston Churchill's steadfast conviction in Britain's ability to overcome Nazi advances inspired a nation. In his position as Prime Minister, Churchill wrote and delivered his now iconic 'We shall never surrender' speech.[38]

His belief, courage, and rousing delivery rallied public morale and laid the groundwork for eventual victory, illustrating how conviction can steer a country through its darkest hours.

Persistence in Action—Apple's Resilience

After Steve Jobs was ousted from Apple in 1985, the company encountered years of dwindling market relevance. However, through persistent innovation and resilience, Apple continued

---

37 (n.d.) 'The British Empire: An Overview.' *BBC.* https://www.bbc.co.uk/bitesize/articles/zpjv3j6#zk9k8hv.
38 Roberts, A. (2018). *Churchill: Walking with Destiny.* Viking.

Chapter 7: C3P3 in Action

to push boundaries. When Jobs returned in 1997, his relentless drive led to the creation of groundbreaking products such as the iMac, iPod, iPhone, and iPad, ultimately marking a triumphant resurgence and underscoring the power of persistence.

Pivot in Action—Netflix's Transformation

As we know, Netflix was originally a DVD rental service. But when it faced fierce competition, new technology, and changing consumer preferences, Netflix boldly pivoted from its traditional business model to fully embrace and invest in new streaming technology. This agile transformation countered emerging threats and positioned Netflix as a global leader in entertainment.[39]

Part-With in Action—Kodak's Missed Opportunity

Unlike Netflix, when faced with a crisis, Kodak didn't respond as well, and its ultimate decline serves as a cautionary tale about the perils of clinging to obsolete strategies. Despite inventing the first digital camera, Kodak refused to part with its legacy film business. And its reluctance to embrace digital technology resulted in a dramatic loss of market dominance.

Sometimes, success requires letting go. Kodak's example highlights the critical importance of timely strategic detachment.

---

39 Meyer. No Rules.

PART 3: Applying C3P3 to Leadership, Strategy, and Performance

Practical Strategies for Leadership

Effective leadership hinges on more than adhering to principles. It also requires actionable strategies. These include:

Communicating with clarity. Maintain transparency by delivering frequent, honest updates to employees, customers, investors, and the public. An informed team is better equipped to deal with a crisis, and respond positively to an opportunity.

Staying calm and focused. Leaders must remain composed under pressure. A calm demeanour helps you to think clearly and make more rational decisions because it keeps you focused on the present and tapped into your logical thinking brain, while also easing negative emotions. It also sets a positive example for the organisation.

Prioritising key issues. In leadership, it's essential to triage. Triaging in business means concentrating on resolving the most critical problems first. Direct your resources towards high-priority challenges and opportunities immediately, leaving those that are less vital for later resolution. In all situations, you also need to understand and prepare for the fact that some issues may require long-term attention.

Fostering collaboration. No leader (not even the best leader) operates well single-handedly. You must learn to delegate responsibilities, encourage team input, and leverage the diverse skills within the organisation to navigate through the ups and downs of leadership, but particularly leadership through crisis.

Adapting and evolving. As a leader, you need to be prepared to regularly reassess the situation and adjust your strategies as new information emerges. Flexibility is vital for long-term resilience and recovery.

> Effective leadership requires actionable strategies.

Integrating C3P3 into Your Leadership Decision-Making

A leader who leverages the C3P3 Framework makes decisions that are both principled and pragmatic because this approach ensures:

- **Balanced ethical considerations.** Grounding actions in character while meeting operational needs to maintain your purpose.
- **Decisive, transparent action.** Harnessing courage to act swiftly in uncertainty.

- **Alignment with long-term vision.** Using conviction to keep all efforts tied to strategic goals.
- **Resilience in the face of adversity.** Relying on persistence to drive progress despite setbacks.
- **Agility to adapt.** Employing pivot to shift strategies as new challenges arise.
- **Strategic detachment.** Utilising part-with to eliminate practices that hinder growth.

A leader who leverages the C3P3 Framework makes decisions that are both principled and pragmatic.

By integrating these elements into your leadership approach, you can become the steady hands guiding your organisations. You will not only steer your teams with clarity and confidence but also lay the groundwork for enduring success.

Crisis in the Dust: Character and Command in Chaos

On 30 May 2007, elements of Task Force Fury (approximately 2,000 ISAF and Afghan National Army troops—including around

Chapter 7: C3P3 in Action

1,000 British soldiers—500 Afghan troops, and other NATO and coalition elements) participated in a British-led NATO air assault known as Operation Lastay Kulang (or Operation Packaxe-Handle). The operation was tasked with striking in the Helmand Province, Afghanistan, with the objective of disrupting Taliban forces that threatened the security and stability of the Lower Sangin Valley.

This area was one of the most dangerous strongholds of Taliban insurgency, and Operation Lastay Kulang demanded precision, coordination, and above all, resilience from everyone involved. Task Force Fury itself was a composite unit, primarily built around the 4th Brigade Combat Team of the 82nd Airborne Division, and it brought a formidable capability to the battlefield.

However, no matter the preparation, skills, or capabilities of the task force, this was always a risky endeavour, and during the initial insertion, a U.S. Army CH-47 Chinook helicopter, call sign Flipper 75, was tragically shot down. All seven on board were killed.

I remember the moment vividly. Watching in disbelief as the aircraft fell from the sky, I felt the confusion rippling through the others in the assault force. The darkness of early morning only added to the chaos, cloaking the battlefield in shadows and uncertainty. Ground forces were already engaged with enemy fighters, but Special Forces teams immediately diverted towards the crash site to secure the area and recover our fallen soldiers.

PART 3: Applying C3P3 to Leadership, Strategy, and Performance

The situation escalated quickly, erupting into a chaotic, multi-domain fight. Firefights flared across the valley, Apache AH-64 helicopters took heavy fire from RPGs and hostile small arms, and radio chatter filled the air with urgent updates and conflicting signals. One Apache pilot later told me that amid the chaos his aircraft was running low on fuel, a warning light blinking, but he refused to abandon the ground troops at the crash site until the relieving aircraft arrived. He stayed because character and conviction demanded nothing less.

This moment became a crucible for leadership—not of a single leader, but of many. The Air Mission Commander, Air Element Commander, Ground Force Commander, and a web of supporting leaders across the fighting domains and services rose together, united in purpose. Each brought their expertise, made split-second decisions, and showed incredible courage, clarity, and persistence in the face of overwhelming noise and danger. They didn't falter. They pivoted, recalibrated, and adapted, and despite the shock of losing Flipper 75, the leadership, and therefore the operation, did not pause. In fact, it accelerated.

The battlefield became a layered battlespace, supported by Predator UAV drone live feeds providing real-time intelligence, fighter jets delivering precision strikes, and Spectre gunships circling overhead. The AC-130 gunship, known as the Spectre, was a heavily armed, long-endurance aircraft, which brought unmatched firepower backed up by about eight hours of loiter time (the phase of flight consisting of flying over a very small region). Armed with side-firing cannons, howitzers, and precision munitions, it could engage targets near friendly forces with devastating accuracy. And during Operation Pickaxe-Handle it was an airborne guardian in the night, its presence as reassuring to our side as it was lethal to the other.

Commanders on the ground and in the air fought through confusion as one cohesive unit. This wasn't about executing a flawless plan, and no one did. But it was about leadership under fire, making decisions amid uncertainty, chaos, and loss.

This is what crisis leadership looks like—not control, but command through character; not perfection, but persistence through chaos; not the absence of fear, but courage in its presence. And most of all, the conviction that the mission must continue, because it simply cannot fail.

Conclusion

You cannot be an influential leader if you can't lead when things don't go to plan. But the ability to make sound decisions under pressure while upholding your purpose, maintaining your ethical standards, and steering the organisation towards long-term success requires mastery of the six C3P3 pillars.

PART 3: Applying C3P3 to Leadership, Strategy, and Performance

As a leader who embraces the pillars of character, courage, conviction, persistence, pivot, and part-with you'll be much better prepared to weather any storm and help your organisation emerge stronger, more resilient, and poised for future success.

CHAPTER 8

Practical Application of C3P3 Leadership with the GROW Model

In organisations, teams are each a distinct entity—one that functions as a single unit, with shared culture, purpose, goals, and idiosyncrasies.[40] But within every cohesive team, we typically find three types of people—those who **can**, those who **can't**, and those who **won't**.

A leader's success is determined not by how they lead the team they wish they had but by how they lead the team they actually have. So it's important to learn how to lead each of these three types of people within a team. And the C3P3 Framework with its

---

40 Benishek, L & Lazzara, E. (9 May 2019). 'Teams in a New Era: Some Considerations and Implications.' *Frontiers in Psychology*. https://pmc.ncbi.nlm.nih.gov/articles/PMC6520615/.

pillars of character, courage, conviction, persisting, pivoting, and parting-with will help you do that well.

A leader's success is determined not by how they lead the team they wish they had but by how they lead the team they actually have.

How to GROW with C3P3

As an overarching step, however, you might want to consider employing the **GROW** model with your team development and leadership. This model is a proven coaching and solution-focused tool that helps individuals and teams achieve their potential by working through four key stages:

- **G**oal—What do we need to achieve?
- **R**eality—Where are we now?
- **O**ptions—What can we do?
- **W**ay forward—What actions will we take?

The GROW model was developed by Sir John Whitmore in the 1980s, and it is still one of the most widely used coaching

Chapter 8: Practical Application of C3P3 Leadership with the GROW Model

frameworks in executive leadership today.[41] It's fantastic. But when you integrate C3P3 principles with the GROW model, you will really maximise performance, address skill gaps, and better foster a high-performing culture overall.

The GROW Model

Source: Coaching Culture at Work [42]

---

41 Performance Consultants. (n.d.). The GROW model. https://www.performanceconsultants.com/resources/the-grow-model/.
42 Coaching Culture At Work. (n.d.) 'The GROW Model.' https://www.coachingcultureatwork.com/the-grow-model/.

PART 3: Applying C3P3 to Leadership, Strategy, and Performance

Understanding the Three Types of Team Members

Before we can understand the application of the GROW Model and the C3P3 Framework, we first need to understand the three types of team members that we'll be dealing with.

1. The People Who Can

The people who *can* are everyone's favourite team members. These individuals are the backbone of any successful team—high performers who consistently deliver results, demonstrate initiative, and uphold the highest standards of professionalism.

These are the performers that don't just meet expectations but consistently exceed them and typically set the benchmark for excellence within their teams and the wider organisation. They have the ability to adapt and solve problems independently, think critically, and drive outcomes—and this makes them invaluable to the team's success.

The challenge with leading people who *can* is that we can sometimes over rely on them, consciously or unconsciously, and give them a disproportionate workload, trusting them to 'get things done' while others underperform.

Being so capable means these individuals can handle greater responsibility, but when we constantly increase their workload

Chapter 8: Practical Application of C3P3 Leadership with the GROW Model

without the right recognition or support, this can lead to frustration, disengagement, and even burnout. In fact, research shows that high performers are particularly vulnerable to burnout with 76% of employees experiencing this sometimes and 28% experiencing it very often.[43]

Conversely, the opposite problem can occur. High performers can sometimes be overlooked or neglected by leaders whose focus, energy, and resources are pulled away by underperforming team members and the need to bring them up to standard. While this is going on, top performers are left to their own devices, receiving little feedback, mentorship, or development opportunities. It's the old 'squeaky wheel gets the grease' problem, and though it's perhaps a normal reaction, it's not a good way to build a successful team. Without meaningful challenges, professional growth, or acknowledgement of their contributions, these individuals may feel undervalued and seek opportunities elsewhere.

To retain and motivate your high-performing 'people who *can*', you must strike a balance. That is making sure that these individuals are recognised, supported, and challenged without overburdening them or making them feel that their contributions are being taken for granted.

---

43 Wigert, B. (13 March 2020). 'Employee Burnout: The Biggest Myth.' Gallup. https://www.gallup.com/workplace/288539/employee-burnout-biggest-myth.aspx.

PART 3: Applying C3P3 to Leadership, Strategy, and Performance

Applying the GROW Model and C3P3 Framework to Leading 'People who Can'

Case study—Balancing the Scales

At a mid-sized financial advisory firm, the Managing Director (MD) noticed a troubling imbalance within his team. One of the junior consultants, David, was pulling far more than his weight, shouldering 40% more work than his peers.

Despite this high workload, he was consistently delivering high-quality results. He was often the first to arrive and the last to leave and sometimes would work well into the night and long after the other team members. Meanwhile, others in the team seemed to be coasting. They were underperforming and failing to meet basic expectations.

The MD knew that they had to make a change. But he also knew that he had to rebalance the scales in a way that supported both David and the broader team.

The Path to Change

Through one-on-one coaching and using the **GROW model** and the **C3P3 Framework**, the MD implemented a structured leadership response:

1. **Goal:** Redistribute workloads to prevent burnout while maintaining high performance.

2. **Reality:** David, a 'person who *can*' performer, was shouldering 40% more work than his peers, leading to frustration and exhaustion. Meanwhile, some team members were underutilised or underperforming.

3. **Leadership tools:**

    - **Character:** The MD acknowledged that letting David carry the team was poor leadership, and it was also unfair and unsustainable. He upheld the values of integrity and fairness and made the call to address the imbalance head-on.

    - **Courage:** It wasn't easy. Having tough conversations with both David and the underperformers was tricky. The MD had to challenge the status quo and confront the reality of the imbalance with courage.

    - **Conviction:** The MD didn't just settle for surface-level fixes. His goal was to create a high-performing yet equitable team, so he was resolute in fostering accountability and ensuring every team member contributed meaningfully.

4. **Options:**

    - Support outcome-focused collaborative conversations between team members, intentionally adjusting communication styles to improve understanding and effort across the team.

- Provide coaching and development for underperformers.
- Restructure assignments based on leadership profile assessments to leverage team strengths.
- Introduce performance-based incentives to encourage balanced contributions.

5. **Way Forward:**
   - **Persist:** Reinforce clear expectations and provide structured coaching across the team.
   - **Pivot:** Implement a peer mentorship program allowing team members to learn from each other and improve skill development.
   - **Part-with:** The MD made the tough decision to eliminate outdated work practices and, where necessary, address underperformance through reassignment or transition.

Outcome: A Balanced, High-Performing Team

By leading with tools from C3P3 and GROW, the MD successfully restructured the team with incredible outcomes, including:

- David remained engaged and improved his work-life balance.
- Underperforming team members reengaged with

the team, sharing the load and delivering improved performance over time, backed by mentorship and coaching.
- The firm cultivated a culture of shared accountability, enhancing productivity, morale, and long-term retention.

Ultimately, the combination of leadership assessments with skill sets and team dynamics allowed for smarter leadership decisions, reinforcing the firm's commitment to excellence, fairness, and sustainable performance.

2. The People Who Can't

The second type of people on our teams are the 'people who *can't.*' These are individuals who have the right mindset and energy but simply lack the skills, experience, or confidence to perform at the expected level. Sometimes, they're in the wrong role or lack proper training. And sometimes they just haven't been given the right guidance to succeed.

The challenge with leading a team with 'people who *can't*' is to determine whether they need development or a reassessment of their fit within the organisation.

PART 3: Applying C3P3 to Leadership, Strategy, and Performance

Applying the GROW Model and C3P3 Framework to Leading 'People who Can't'

Case Study: Nurturing Leadership Growth in a Rapid Expansion

When a tier-one engineering firm landed a major contract, it triggered a period of rapid expansion, including a big restructure. During the restructuring process, Sarah, who was widely recognised as an industry-leading engineer and hugely celebrated for her technical expertise, was promoted to a state manager role and suddenly found herself overseeing a team of 30.

While Sarah was highly skilled in the firm's core business, she had minimal leadership experience, and her new job brought an entirely different set of challenges. She had little experience managing people, navigating strategy, or engaging with government and other external stakeholders, all of which were core parts of her new position.

On top of those challenges, the speed of the expansion shifted the team dynamics literally overnight, and there was limited change management in place. This left many in the team feeling unsettled, uncertain, unsupported, and unclear in the team's (and organisation's) direction. Sarah was not equipped with the skills to manage this, and within the first year under Sarah's leadership, nine team members resigned, citing frustrations with her communication and leadership styles.

Sarah hadn't failed. But she had been promoted without the preparation and support needed to fully step into her leadership role.

The Path to Change

1. **Goal:** Support Sarah to grow into her new leadership role and develop the needed capabilities, particularly in communication, delegation, and team and stakeholder engagement.

2. **Reality**: Sarah's technical expertise was never in question, but her lack of leadership experience led to communication breakdowns, team dissatisfaction, and attrition. Leadership assessments provided critical insights into the leadership traits that were not yet evident in Sarah's approach.

3. **The Leadership Response:**

    o **Character**—The CEO approached Sarah's situation with empathy, recognising that her struggle was not due to a lack of effort or intent but rather an absence of leadership training and experience. Rather than assigning blame, the CEO chose to understand and invest in her growth.

    o **Courage**—Honest and direct conversations were held with Sarah regarding the impact of her leadership style on team morale. The CEO didn't shy away from addressing the resignations and their root causes. And she created space for reflection and growth.

- **Conviction**—The CEO engaged me to conduct a number of assessments to identify individual and team communication styles and ensure they're aligned with the overall team purpose. These assessments helped reveal both strengths and friction points in working styles.

4. **Options:**

    - **Persisting**—Sarah began one-on-one leadership coaching and attended facilitated team workshops. These helped Sarah and her team adjust their communication styles for more effective collaboration and solution-focused conversations. The support was structured, consistent, and focused on providing real behavioural change.

    - **Pivoting**—Rather than removing Sarah from the role, the organisation invested in her development, choosing to equip her to grow into it. With coaching, tools, and a better understanding of her team, they started to build better flow within the team and develop strong leadership capabilities.

    - **Parting-with**—In this case, Sarah was able to grow into the role she had. But had she been unable or unwilling to adapt, the organisation would have considered a transition back to a technical role. And that would have been okay as well.

5. **Way Forward:**

    o The firm decided to persist, implementing structured coaching for Sarah, using the GROW model to refine her leadership style.

    o The team adjusted their communication styles based on assessment insights, improving overall dynamics and productivity.

    o Sarah developed a more confident and strategic approach to leadership, enhancing engagement with government stakeholders and ensuring better task delegation within her team.

Outcome: Leadership Evolution and Team Stability

With targeted development and a structured support system, Sarah grew into a confident, capable leader. Communication across the team improved. Morale lifted. And work became more efficient. Several team members who had previously resigned returned to the newly invigorated team, positioning the team for long-term success.

By applying the GROW Model, alongside the principles of C3P3, the organisation didn't just salvage a leadership appointment. They built something even better. And Sarah didn't just stay in the firm—she stepped up to the plate and started hitting home runs. In doing so she helped stabilise the team, retain talent, and position the business for future success, proving that the right support can turn a struggling leader into a thriving one.

3. The People Who Won't

The third group of people that you'll likely have on your team is 'people who *won't*'. These are individuals who have the skills but consistently choose not to apply them. Often they are resistant to change or lack motivation, and they may even actively disrupt progress. For these individuals, it's not about capability, it's about attitude. And that makes these cases one of the most challenging leadership tasks.

Applying the GROW Model and C3P3 Framework to Leading 'People Who Won't'

Case Study—Navigating Resistance to Strengthen Team Culture

At a large organisation, the CEO was preparing her team for the organisation's signature marketing event—a high-energy, 14-hour day that was expected to generate much-needed leads.

Each team member had a role to play and was assigned specific responsibilities. The goal wasn't just to secure leads but also to reinforce team cohesion and collaboration.

Unfortunately, one long-serving team member simply refused

Chapter 8: Practical Application of C3P3 Leadership with the GROW Model

to engage. His role was to manage stakeholder engagement, a key role in the event's success. But instead of contributing, he isolated himself from the team and openly stated, *'I'm not doing this.'* While the rest of the team worked hard, pushing outside of their comfort zones, his resistance created tension, lowered morale, and directly impacted outcomes.

The Path to Change

1. **Goal:** Create a team environment where everyone contributes with shared commitment, especially during high-impact events.
2. **Reality:** This individual had the experience and the skills but was disengaged and resistant. During the event he avoided taking on his responsibilities and assigned tasks, and his behaviour disrupted the team, lowered morale and engagement, and set a poor example.
3. **The Leadership Response:**
    - **Character**—The CEO did not ignore the issue but addressed the behaviour directly, checking in with the individual to understand his resistance.
    - **Courage**—Honest, one-on-one conversations were held post-event to discuss his lack of engagement and refusal to perform assigned duties. Support was offered, but the attitude persisted. The CEO made it clear that there were boundaries and expectations that had to be met.

- **Conviction**—Performance expectations were reinforced fairly and consistently. Everyone else was showing up and he couldn't be the exception. However, weeks later, he made inappropriate comments to a colleague, making them feel uncomfortable. A direct conversation followed, making it clear that such behaviour was unacceptable.

4. **Options:** The CEO engaged me to conduct individual behaviour and personality assessments to identify the team member's work style, engagement levels, and behavioural impact.

    - **Persisting:** Individual coaching sessions were arranged, but his negative attitude continued. Ultimately, he refused to take advantage of multiple coaching opportunities offered to him.
    - **Pivoting:** Other team members refused to work alongside him due to his ongoing disengagement and poor performance. Despite attempts to reposition him in a role that aligned better with his mindset, he showed no willingness to adapt.
    - **Parting-with:** In the end, following due process and policy, it became evident he would not transition into an 'I can' team member. The CEO made the call to

exit him from the organisation. It wasn't personal—it was about protecting team morale, culture, and organisational effectiveness.

5. **Way Forward:** The organisation moved forward with stronger clarity around team expectations and more cohesive team values. The CEO's decision reinforced that behaviour and attitude matter just as much as capability. She also showed that the leadership would stand firm when it counts.

Outcome—A Stronger, More Aligned Team

By leading with conviction and holding firm on accountability, the CEO prevented one individual's negativity from derailing the whole team. The event was still a success. And in the end, team morale was preserved, the team felt supported, and a culture of shared responsibility and performance expectations was reinforced.

> Sometimes, the best leadership decision is the hardest one.

Sometimes, the best leadership decision is the hardest one. But by combining the GROW Model with the C3P3 pillars, the organisation was able to implement a firm, fair, and structured approach to managing conflict and setting a culture for a healthy, high-performing team.

Taking Decisive Action as a Leader

As these case studies showcase, the integration of C3P3 with the GROW model gives leaders a structured yet flexible approach to tackling performance challenges while maintaining fairness, accountability, and a strong team culture. If you're keen to implement this within your own teams, start with the following:

1. **Identify where each team member stands**—Are they a **can**, **can't**, or **won't**?
2. **Apply the C3P3 principles** to determine the best course of action.
3. **Use the GROW model** to facilitate structured conversations, development plans, and, if necessary, exit strategies.
4. **Be courageous and consistent**—Do not let one team member's issues derail overall team success.
5. **Lead with integrity and fairness**—Ensure decisions are guided by values, not convenience or emotion.

Conclusion

Leadership is not about perfection. The best leaders lead the team they have, not the team they wish they had, and instead of bemoaning the situation, look to develop potential, address gaps, and remove obstacles to success.

Chapter 8: Practical Application of C3P3 Leadership with the GROW Model

By mastering the C3P3 framework and applying the GROW model with precision, leaders can navigate the complexities of people management, and help their teams operate with clarity, confidence, and a commitment to excellence.

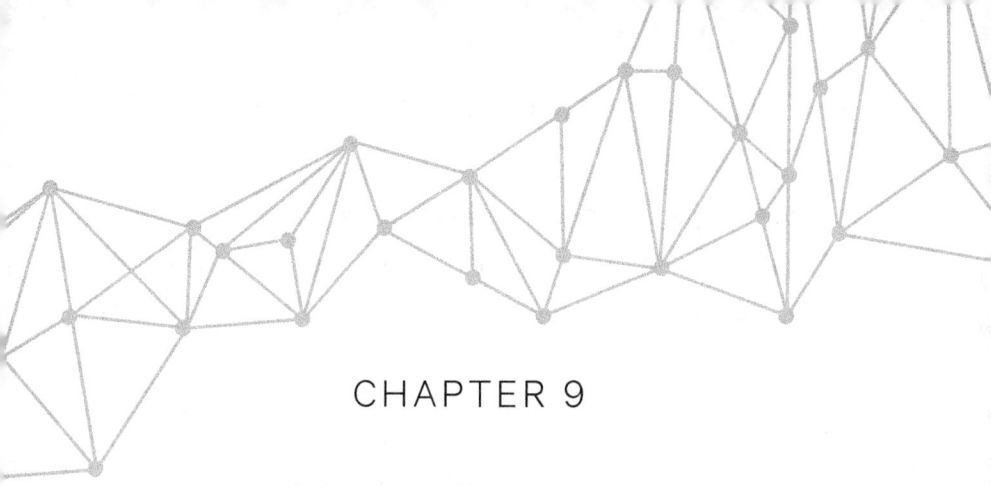

CHAPTER 9

The C3P3 Leader

You've travelled the C3P3 path quite a long way—through challenge, insight, and personal reflection. But this isn't the end of your journey. It's just the beginning. Because leadership, after all, isn't a destination—it's a way of being. It's a mindset. It's a continual evolution shaped by experience, reflection, and action.

> Because leadership, after all, isn't a destination— it's a way of being.

Throughout this book, you've explored what it means to lead with **character**, **courage**, and **conviction**, and to embody the practices of **persistence**, **pivoting**, and **parting-with**. These six elements form the C3P3 framework and are your blueprint for becoming a leader who not only drives performance but is also influential.

Becoming a C3P3 leader is not about ticking boxes or reaching a final form. It's about committing to the lifelong journey of leadership—one driven by purpose, adaptability, and meaningful impact to deliver incredible results in your own leadership as well as those around you.

Embedding the C3P3 Framework into Your Leadership

The best leaders don't stop once they've 'learned' something. Even masters are continually challenging themselves. To sustain your development as a C3P3 leader, you have to build habits around the practice, and that begins with intentional self-assessment.

> The best leaders don't stop once they've 'learned' something.

Here are four strategies to guide your growth:

1. Practice Regular Self-Reflection

Check in with yourself regularly. Take time to evaluate your actions, decisions, and behaviours. This ongoing habit fosters self-awareness, helps identify areas for growth, and ensures your leadership aligns with your values and vision.

2. Ask for Real Feedback

Invite honest input from peers, mentors, and team members. Ask them how they see you showing up and particularly how you're going with applying the C3P3 Framework. Growth requires humility and the willingness to listen and adjust. Feedback is fuel—there for you to use to improve.

3. Make a Leadership Development Plan

Map out your goals and the steps needed to strengthen each C3P3 element. Pick one area that you want to work on, then break it down and set a goal with practical actions attached. Be sure to set timelines, track your progress, and flexibly adjust your plan as you evolve. Small shifts can lead to big changes over time.

PART 3: Applying C3P3 to Leadership, Strategy, and Performance

4. Commit to Continuous Learning

Leadership isn't static. Stay curious and open to new perspectives. Read, attend workshops, and connect with mentors. Great leaders are always learning.

Building the Kind of Leadership Legacy that Outlives You

At its core, leadership is about more than just results—it's about the impact you leave behind. And the ultimate goal of leadership is to leave a legacy, one that transcends your individual achievements and empowers others to lead with integrity and vision.

How can you do that?

> Leadership is about more than just results—it's about the impact you leave behind.

Mentor Future Leaders

Share your experience. Invest in those around you. Encourage others to grow into their own leadership potential.

Foster a C3P3 Culture

Create a culture where the principles of C3P3 are lived out daily. Where character, courage, and conviction are valued, and where people feel safe to challenge the status quo, grow, and contribute.

Lead by Example

Your actions will always speak louder than your words. Model the behaviours you hope to inspire in others. Be the leader others look to in times of uncertainty.

The C3P3 Mindset: Leadership That Lasts

Leadership isn't about power, position, or prestige. It's about influence, service, and legacy. The C3P3 framework serves as a compass, guiding you when the path is unclear, grounding you in values, and pushing you towards bold, principled action.

- **Character** anchors your decisions.
- **Courage** drives you forward.
- **Conviction** keeps you aligned.
- **Persistence** carries you through adversity.
- **Pivoting** helps you adapt with agility.
- **Parting-with** gives you the freedom to let go of what no longer serves.

These are not just leadership traits—they are life practices. Adopt them fully, and they will shape not only your leadership but also your legacy.

Where to From Here?

Leadership is not without its challenges. It will test you. There will be moments of doubt, late nights, tough calls, high-stakes decisions, and the pressure to get things right. That's just part of the package. But true leadership doesn't emerge from perfection—you won't always get it right. It isn't about doing things right. It's about doing the right things. Keep showing up with authenticity, making tough calls with integrity, and empowering others to do the same.

You now have everything you need to lead with character, courage, and conviction. To persist through obstacles, pivot when necessary, and part with what holds you back.

The C3P3 framework is yours to use, to refine, and to pass on to your emerging leaders, teams, and organisations. You have everything you need to leave a leadership legacy that will endure beyond your tenure.

You have everything you need to leave a leadership legacy that will endure beyond your tenure.

So take the first step. Then the next step. And the next. The challenge is yours. The future is yours. Lead it with purpose. Lead it with impact. Leave a legacy worth following.

— Andrew

Work with Andrew

In today's fast-paced and ever-evolving business landscape, leadership demands more than just technical expertise; it requires strategic insight, critical reflection, decisive action, and continuous improvement to be truly influential.

Andrew Middleton brings over three decades of leadership experience within the military and corporate environments. His vision is to empower today's leaders to influence and develop the next generation.

At the core of Andrew's leadership and business performance consulting is the C3P3 Framework, a practical leadership model grounded in character, courage, conviction, persistence, pivoting, and parting-with. This framework is amplified by advanced tools such as Hogan, DISC Advanced, and The GC Index, enabling clients to sharpen their leadership, build resilient and impactful teams, and achieve sustainable growth.

Andrew's expertise has been instrumental in building influential leadership capabilities across various industries. His clients value his ability to bridge military operational leadership with real-world business strategy—challenging assumptions, cutting through complexity, and delivering practical outcomes.

Get in touch with Andrew's team at:
info@middletonconsultinggroup.com or +61 0487 777 296.

Alternatively, jump onto Andrew's website at: https://middletonconsultinggroup.com/ to find out about his coaching programs and workshops.

Middleton Consulting Group's Services

Leadership & Organisational Transformation Assessments

Leadership Coaching & Mentoring

Team Performance & Organisational Leadership Programs

To explore how Andrew and Middleton Consulting Group can support your leadership journey and organisational goals, book a consultation at:
https://middletonconsultinggroup.com/contact/.

Bibliography

Anthony, S et al. (2008). *The Innovator's Guide to Growth: Putting Disruptive Innovation to Work.* Harvard Business Review Press.

Aran, Y & Pollman, E. (3 November 2023). 'Ousted.' *Theoretical Inquiries in Law.* https://papers.ssrn.com/sol3/papers.cfm?abstract_id=4625990.

BBC. 'The British Empire: An Overview.' https://www.bbc.co.uk/bitesize/articles/zpjv3j6#zk9k8hv.

Benishek, L & Lazzara, E. (9 May 2019). 'Teams in a New Era: Some Considerations and Implications.' *Frontiers in Psychology.* https://pmc.ncbi.nlm.nih.gov/articles/PMC6520615/.

Berger, C. (21 May 2024). 'Satya Nadella transformed Microsoft's culture during his decade as CEO by turning everyone into 'learn-it-alls' instead of 'know-it-alls.' *Fortune.* https://fortune.com/2024/05/20/satya-nadella-microsoft-culture-growth-mindset-learn-it-alls-know-it-alls/.

Bradberry. T. (7 December 2015). 'Why the best leaders have conviction.' World Economic Forum. https://www.weforum.org/stories/2015/12/why-the-best-leaders-have-conviction/.

Branson, R. (2009). *Richard Branson: Losing my Virginity.* Virgin Books.

Cavaness, K, Picchioni, A & Fleshman, JW. (3 June 2020). 'Linking Emotional Intelligence to Successful Health Care Leadership: The Big Five Model of Personality.' *Clinics in Colon and Rectal Surgery.* https://pmc.ncbi.nlm.nih.gov/articles/PMC7329378/.

Chen, H & Lin, Y. (July 2018). 'Goal orientations, leader-leader exchange, trust, and the outcomes of project performance.' *International Journal of Project Management.* https://www.sciencedirect.com/science/article/abs/pii/S0263786317303174.

Clark, D. (2016). *Alibaba: The house that Jack Ma built.* Harper Collins US.

Coaching Culture At Work. (n.d.) 'The GROW Model.' https://www.coachingcultureatwork.com/the-grow-model/.

Colby, L. (2015). *Road to Power: How GM's Mary Barra Shattered the Glass Ceiling.* Wiley.

Conviction. (2025). In Cambridge University Press & Assessment 2025. https://dictionary.cambridge.org/dictionary/english/conviction.

Curry, D. (18 February 2025). 'Apple Statistics (2025).' Business of Apps. https://www.businessofapps.com/data/apple-statistics/.

de Jong, E. (12 December 2021). 'Fractious Australia has much to learn from the kindness and purpose of New Zealand politics.' *The Guardian.* https://www.theguardian.com/commentisfree/2021/dec/12/fractious-australia-has-much-to-learn-from-the-kindness-and-purpose-of-new-zealand-politics.

Dweck, C. (14 January 2016). 'What Having a "Growth Mindset" Actually Means.' *Harvard Business Review.* https://hbr.org/2016/01/what-having-a-growth-mindset-actually-means.

Eurich, T. (5 January 2018). 'What Self-Awareness Really Is (and How to Cultivate It).' *Harvard Business Review.* https://hbr.org/2018/01/what-self-awareness-really-is-and-how-to-cultivate-it.

Fell, J. (30 September 2023). 'Netflix's DVD business almost didn't exist. Twenty-five years on, it has transformed the media industry.'

Bibliography

News. https://www.abc.net.au/news/2023-09-30/netflix-shutters-dvd-delivery-marc-randolph/102902864.

Fink, S. (1986). *Crisis Management: Planning for the Inevitable*. American Management Association.

Franklin, J. (2011). *The 33: The Ultimate Account of the Chilean Miners Dramatic Rescue*. Transworld Digital.

Gallo, A. (15 February 2023). 'What Is Psychological Safety?' *Harvard Business Review*. https://hbr.org/2023/02/what-is-psychological-safety.

Garrido-Moreno, A, Martín-Rojas, R & García-Morales, V. (August 2024). 'The key role of innovation and organizational resilience in improving business performance: A mixed-methods approach.' *International Journal of Information Management*. https://www.sciencedirect.com/science/article/pii/S0268401224000252.

Howell, E. (27 April 2022). 'SpaceX: Facts about Elon Musk's private spaceflight company.' Space.com. https://www.space.com/18853-spacex.html.

Huddleston, T. (29 April 2024). 'Richard Branson says this decision helped build his $2.5B net worth: "I don't think I would have gone to space' otherwise."' *CNBC*. https://www.cnbc.com/2024/04/29/richard-branson-tough-business-decision-helped-me-build-virgin-group.html.

Iger, R. (2019). *The Ride of a Lifetime: Lessons in Creative Leadership from 15 Years as CEO of Walt Disney Company*. Random House.

Isaacson, W. (2011). *Steve Jobs*. Simon & Schuster.

Kahney, L. (2019). *Tim Cook: The Genius Who Took Apple to the Next Level*. Portfolio.

Bibliography

Knoff, D. (2022). *537 Days of Winter: Resilience, endurance and humanity while stranded in Antarctica during the pandemic.* Affirm Press.

le Cunff, A. (28 December 2023). 'Ness Labs: The Art and Science of Letting Go.' Ness Labs. https://newsletter.nesslabs.com/posts/ness-labs-the-art-and-science-of-letting-go#:~:text=We%20also%20tend%20to%20cling,similar%20situations%20in%20the%20future.

Lewis, A. (26 October 2022). 'Good Leadership? It All Starts With Trust.' Harvard Business Publishing. https://www.harvardbusiness.org/good-leadership-it-all-starts-with-trust/.

McCarthy, K, O'Connell, D & Hall, D. (September 2005). 'Leading beyond tragedy: The balance of personal identity and adaptability.' *Leadership & Organization Development Journal.* https://www.researchgate.net/publication/242348015_Leading_beyond_tragedy_The_balance_of_personal_identity_and_adaptability.

Meyer, E & Hastings, R. (2020). *No Rules: Netflix and the Culture of Reinvention.* Penguin Press.

Nancarrow, D. (2015). *Game Changer: How John Borghetti changed the face of aviation in Australia.* HarperSports AU.

Performance Consultants. (n.d.). The GROW model. https://www.performanceconsultants.com/resources/the-grow-model/.

Richter, F. (21 December 2016). 'Apple's Growth Since Re-Hiring Steve Jobs 20 Years Ago.' statista. https://www.statista.com/chart/7330/apple-revenue-since-1997/.

Roberts, A. (2018). *Churchill: Walking with Destiny.* Viking.

Rometty, G. (2023). *Good Power: Leading Positive Change in Our Lives, Work, and World.* Harvard Business Review Press.

Bibliography

Simone, F. (4 December 2017). 'Negative Self-Talk: Don't Let It Overwhelm You.' *Psychology Today.* https://www.psychologytoday.com/au/blog/family-affair/201712/negative-self-talk-dont-let-it-overwhelm-you.

Stone, B. (2021). *Amazon Unbound: Jeff Bezos and the invention of a global empire.* Simon & Schuster.

Sutton, J. (3 January 2019). 'What Is Resilience & Why Is It Important to Bounce Back?' *Positive Psychology.* https://positivepsychology.com/what-is-resilience/.

Taylor, E, Shirouzu, N & White, J. (22 July 2020). 'How Tesla defined a new era for the global auto industry.' Reuters. https://www.reuters.com/article/technology/how-tesla-defined-a-new-era-for-the-global-auto-industry-idUSKCN24N0GB/#:~:text=Tesla%20would%20go%20on%20to,radical%20thinking%20and%20fast%20innovation.

Weinberg, R. (3 January 2013). 'Mental toughness: What is it and how to build it.' *Revista da Educação Física.* https://www.researchgate.net/publication/262665458_Mental_toughness_What_is_it_and_how_to_build_it/citation/download.

Wigert, B. (13 March 2020). 'Employee Burnout: The Biggest Myth.' Gallup. https://www.gallup.com/workplace/288539/employee-burnout-biggest-myth.aspx.

www.ingramcontent.com/pod-product-compliance
Lightning Source LLC
Chambersburg PA
CBHW071241070526
44583CB00017B/2276

PRAISE FOR *Refilled*

"If you've ever suffered a soul-deep ache and wondered why you can't seem to access the fullness referred to in Scripture, look no further than this book. *Refilled* will not only minister to those deep places of longing, but it will equip you with spiritual insights and tools to move forward. Kristine has the unique gift of not only being a wonderful Bible teacher, but unearthing scriptural treasures in new, profound ways. Her insights into the life of Naomi left me wanting to pick up my Bible and dig into this rich story of God's redemption and refilling. This is a book I will be recommending to others for years to come."

    ABBY MCDONALD, author of *Shift*, writing coach,
    and contributor for Proverbs 31 Ministries

"I've always been in awe of Kristine's gift of opening the Bible and showing us that we aren't alone in our struggles. The way she digs into Naomi's painful story and finds gems to point out that she experienced what we all face at times: loss, hopelessness, loneliness. But she doesn't leave us there. She also shows us how God was there to fill the void in Naomi's life, and he'll fill ours too. Grief hits hard and as a special needs mom, it's ongoing in my life. No matter how heavy the load is in your own life, this beautiful book will remind us both that God is there and waiting for us to choose him to fulfill us in ways only he can."

    KIM STEWART, marketing strategist,
    host of *Book Marketing Mania* podcast

"Each one of us will experience heartbreak in this life, leaving behind feelings of emptiness only God can fill. In *Refilled*, author Kristine Brown walks readers through the life of a woman in Scripture who experienced her own deep loss. Through that story, Kristine shows us the many ways God will replenish our hearts when we trust him with our emptiness. *Refilled* offers hope for renewal for anyone dealing with the pain of loss and wanting to rediscover a fulfilled life through Christ."

    JODI SNOWDON, author of *Depth: Growing Through Heartbreak to Strength*, host of the *Depth Podcast*

"Kristine's fresh take on Naomi's story helped remind me that God delights in filling up my empty spaces with His goodness. Each chapter of *Refilled* draws from a deep well of biblical wisdom, and these truths refreshed my weary soul. If heartbreaking circumstances have drained you of hope, this reassuring book will flood you with much needed encouragement."

> **LYLI DUNBAR**, writer, biblical life coach, and host of *The Wildfire Faith Podcast*; writer for Proverbs 31 Ministries *First 5 App* and Love God Greatly

"The question I've pondered for years is how God will replace the irreplaceable. Kristine's statement in *Refilled* shed light on this for me: "God being our portion doesn't mean he'll replace what's lost, but his supply will satisfy us in our pain, allowing us to live fulfilled instead of empty." Using biblical characters and her life stories, Kristine gently weaves within each chapter scriptural steps to God's refilling. Through *Refilled*, we learn that living fulfilled is an ongoing process, and God promises to accompany us every step of the way. You will refer to this book over and over. Be sure to add this to your must-read list."

> **CARMEN HORNE**, author, host of *Your Hope Coach* podcast, and board certified life coach

"In *Refilled*, the Scriptures come alive. Author Kristine Brown weaves the biblical story of Naomi into our everyday lives and circumstances. Kristine is a master craftsman carefully creating a tapestry that intertwines our lives with that of Naomi. We feel the aching void that Naomi has in her life. We know her pain, because we have felt it in our own lives. Kristine reminds us that trusting God with our lives and the lives of our loved ones takes practice. In *Refilled*, we learn to rely on God, releasing our bitterness so that God's strength will sustain us. But most importantly, we can look forward to the new ways God will fill our emptiness. And oh, how we will be *Refilled* at that time!"

> **ELLEN CHAUVIN**, author of *Longing to Belong*

"If you feel like something is missing and your heart isn't quite whole, you are not alone. Kristine helps you discover, through the life of Naomi, how God can fill the empty spaces in your heart and live a life *Refilled*. Kristine has written an excellent resource that can be read on your own or used as a study guide with a group of friends."

> **STEPHANIE K. ADAMS**, author of *In the Shadow of the Cross: Following Jesus Through His Last Days*